Intimate Relations

Jacquie Durrell was born in Manchester and studied operatic singing there from the age of seventeen until she left to marry Gerald Durrell. Since her marriage she describes herself as having been secretary, housekeeper, dogsbody, animal keeper, motor mechanic, and general nuisance and chief nagger to her husband. She has been with him on major expeditions to different parts of the world, and organized one separate expedition herself to the Argentine. The Durrells now live in Jersey where Gerald Durrell is Hon. Director of the Jersey Wildlife Preservation Trust.

She retains a strong interest in opera and has an extensive collection of gramophone records. She enjoys cricket, reads voraciously and widely, and is passionately fond of the internal combustion engine. Her previous book, *Beasts in my B____ ___ ____ ____lable in Fontana.

Jacquie Durrell

Intimate Relations

FONTANA/COLLINS

First published by William Collins Sons & Co. Ltd, 1976
First issued in Fontana 1977

Copyright © Jacquie Durrell 1976

Made and printed in Great Britain
by William Collins Sons & Co. Ltd, Glasgow

For Timothy – In deep gratitude for his love and devotion to a far lesser animal.

Contents

List of Illustrations 9

Chapter One Apes and Arias 11

Chapter Two Big-footed Bird 22

Chapter Three Nicotine and Night Monkeys 38

Chapter Four Bullets and Bichos 58

Chapter Five Penguins Galore 74

Chapter Six Small Beef 90

Chapter Seven Fon and Frolics 105

Chapter Eight A Dog's Life 137

Epilogue 159

Illustrations

Eggbert the Screamer
Cai the Douracouli
One of the armadillo twins
Pooh the Crab-eating Raccoon
The Guira Cuckoo
The Fon of Bafut (*Life Magazine*)
N'Pongo the Gorilla
Whiskers the Emperor Tamarin (*Jersey Evening Post*)
Miffy the Spot-nosed Monkey (*Douglas Fisher*)
Timothy the Ground Squirrel (*Jean Mohr*)

Chapter One

Apes and Arias

The only thing that everyone I meet wants to know is how, when and where did I become so involved with animals. Was I perhaps the daughter of a farmer or a vet, or did I study zoology at university? Alas, it was not as straightforward as that.

At the age of seventeen I decided to embark on a musical career, having been assured by several experts that I had an outstanding contralto voice. To begin with my poor father was deeply shocked, having been convinced that either teaching or the law were the right careers for me. Singing, he felt with some reason, was a hazardous profession and lacked security. Such arguments were however not likely to persuade me to change my mind, for I was a natural rebel and loathed anything that savoured of respectability or dullness. A battle of wills began, which I eventually won. The next three years were full of musical theory, interpretation, scales, long practice sessions, followed by the odd appearance at that north-country phenomenon, the musical festival. So there was not a lot of spare time. What there was was taken up by the odd male friend, but nothing serious enough to draw me away from my precious work.

When I was twenty my normally shrewd father, in

the face of far saner advice – mine – suddenly decided to buy a small private hotel for my stepmother to run. Why I will never know, as neither of them had the slightest experience of hotel-keeping or catering, but he was determined to go ahead simply on the score that he had been offered 'a bargain'. This establishment apparently catered not only for the commercial people but also for the theatricals who adorned the Manchester theatres. At the time of our take-over the hotel was full of members of the visiting Sadler's Wells Opera Company and I greatly looked forward to meeting them and, as I hoped, discussing their roles and interpretations and perhaps picking up some useful tips. I was doomed to disappointment for the *only* thing these dear ladies could talk about was an individual called Gerry Durrell – happily absent in Dublin – who, if they were to be believed, was a cross between a Greek god and a well-known American film star, with a bit of St Francis thrown in! I could hardly wait to meet this paragon.

Either I was expecting too much or my initial introduction to Mr Durrell was not in exactly the right circumstances (he was surrounded by fawning females) but I had the distinct impression of a thoroughly spoilt, far-too-good-looking, arrogant young man – definitely not my type at all. When it became obvious to both admirers and admired that I was not impressed I was made the target of ceaseless propaganda. Worse still, on the departure of the operatic ladies, the gentleman himself entered the fray. I was pursued at every turn, bombarded with flowers, invitations to lunch and dinner, to the theatre, the cinema, all supported by an immense battery of charm and wit.

After some time I admit that I was beginning to change my mind. Perhaps, I concluded, I had been a bit hasty and unfair. Still, when the time came for him to leave for Guyana I had a feeling of intense relief. The mixture had been too rich for my taste; pleasant enough for a change but not suitable for a steady diet. To the enquiries of friends and relatives I replied that I had enjoyed Gerry's company but, as I would probably never see him again, no one had anything to worry about, least of all me.

Some time the following year I returned home one afternoon to find Gerry Durrell, drink in hand, regaling my stepmother with funny stories about his latest adventures. I was not only shocked to see him but horrified to hear that he was staying with us until all the animals he had brought to the local zoo had been dispatched to their new owners. On top of this he calmly assumed that I would be overjoyed to see him and only too happy to resume our relationship. My father was far from pleased to see him, never having approved of his liaison with the opera group, so I had hopes that opposition from this quarter would deter friend Durrell. It did not; in fact he demanded to know what objections my father had, whereupon resistance collapsed temporarily at least.

Such was the magic of the man that I soon found myself devoting what spare time I had to being his secretary-cum-business-aide (unpaid naturally), writing out long lists of animals and birds to send to zoos, rushing over to Liverpool to discuss arrangements with shipping lines and agents, paying bills as money came in from animal sales and even sending off personal notes to his anxious mother in Bournemouth. Being freed from this dull routine enabled Gerry to spend more time with his precious animals. I too became involved with them, if only as a spectator, and soon we began often heated discussions on the ethics of catching and selling animals – a subject about which I felt very strongly indeed. Soon Gerry was trying to explain to me how he felt about wild creatures and places. He agreed that the average zoo was a dreadful side-show but maintained that there were good zoos which believed, as he did, that the whole purpose of keeping animals in captivity was to study, breed and save them from the total extinction that was facing them even in those days (1950). That mankind had to be made to realize what would happen was always uppermost in his mind and he was determined that one day he would have his own zoo where his theories about keeping animals, especially those threatened with extinction, could be put into practice. So began my re-education and conversion to the cause of conservation of both animals and wild places, for these two must go hand in hand if either is to be successful.

At this time I still believed there was nothing I wanted to do but to continue with my own career. My family and friends were more sceptical about the degree of my dedication. My father became deeply concerned, even angry. Could I not see where all this was leading? I was getting hopelessly involved with this man who had no job, nor any prospect of getting one. Quite obviously Gerry had no money so why could I be bothering with him unless I were emotionally involved? My father went on and on in this way until we had a blazing row and he forbade me to have anything more to do with this upstart. Gerry heard about all this and had yet another interview with my father, who again backed down. In any case as Gerry was still living in the house it would have been impossible for me to ignore him altogether – and he had not been asked to leave . . .

I think it was my father's rather ridiculous attitude that finally pushed us together. I had long realized that Gerry was a fundamentally different person from the shallow figure he had originally seemed to be. Also he had never made any secret of his feelings for me or his hope that he would persuade me to marry him eventually. So when my father again challenged me to explain my conduct – probably stirred up by local gossip and speculation – my Irish blood fired up. I told him not to be a fool and believe the worst. If he really thought that badly of me, I said, then I would behave badly – and I slammed out of the room. My view was that my father ought to know me far too well to come the heavy-handed Victorian parent. If he wanted to force a situation, then be damned to him!

Our joint finances were not exactly ideal for embarking on matrimony, Gerry having £49 after all his debts had been settled and I about £15. Gerry had inherited £3000 in 1946, but he promptly lost it all by going on three collecting expeditions to the Cameroons and what was then British Guiana. Acting on a mad impulse, however, we decided to leave them all to it and to go down to Bournemouth and Gerry's, we hoped, more understanding family. After the initial excitement of meeting three other Durrells – Mother, Margaret and Leslie (brother Larry being in Yugoslavia) and then the hurried wedding – just in case my irate father appeared – we took stock of our shaky situation. As Margaret owed Gerry some money she suggested we occupy one of the bed-sitters in her house, rent free; that way we could use what money we had to live on. This was a perfect arrangement from my point of view – having the family there without actually living with them. Our small room, 12 ft × 8 ft, was crammed full of stuff – a double bed, one easy chair, a writing table, a chest of drawers and a bookcase. Fortunately there was a tiny fireplace, so heating was no problem. From our one large window we looked out on to the back garden edged with tall pine trees – quite a pleasant change from Manchester.

By careful planning we managed to live on £2.50 a week; Gerry's only luxury being cigarettes, which he rolled himself. There was nothing left after food for anything else so we had to make full use of the rather battered old radio a friend passed on to us, and the local library assumed an important role in our lives. Not only could it supply books to read but it also stocked those newspapers and periodicals that advertised the sort of jobs Gerry was qualified to do – game warden or zoo personnel. A stream of letters went out to all parts of the world, enquiring of all the zoos if they had a vacancy. At that time, however, the game departments were tending to take on only those people who were natives of the area or, at least, local residents so we had no luck there. To increase my worries Gerry then began to have intermittent bouts of malaria which left him completely exhausted.

Our meagre funds had practically run out. We could not get aid from the State as neither of us had ever had full time work in the UK. It was a lowering experience, particularly as many of those to whom Gerry wrote for jobs did not even bother to reply, and so we were both pretty desperate when an old acquaintance of Gerry's asked us to look after a small menagerie for three weeks in Margate. All our living and travel expenses would be covered and there would be a little pocket-money. Naturally we leapt at this opportunity, if only to give us a much needed break from postman-watching.

I found working with animals fascinating. At last I could understand what it meant to Gerry and why he refused to do any other job. The collection was small, consisting mainly of tropical fish, but there were odd birds like Mynahs and Macaws plus a handful of mammals – South American Coatis, West African

Mongooses, a few monkeys and my particular favourite, a fox-red Himalayan Panda. To begin with I was very nervous in case I did anything wrong or let one of the creatures out, but under Gerry's patient, but firm, tuition I soon learned to relax and to develop a simple routine. I was so quick to learn that Gerry complimented me on my natural aptitude, saying I was the best student he had ever taught. Undoubtedly this brief period of indoctrination into the art of looking after animals was of enormous value to me two years later when we began our joint collecting trips. But all too soon this break came to an end when our friend returned. I was heartbroken to leave the animals, even the fish who were delightful to watch, but it had given us a time to reassess our situation and I was still confident that a job would turn up.

So back to Bournemouth we went, to day after day of waiting for the letter that never came and to watching our money disappear. Gerry's family were marvellous, without them we could never have survived so long, but they too were pushed for funds. I found our situation intolerably frustrating and with this feeling came anger, then inspiration. Ever since I had known Gerry he had entertained and captivated me with stories about the animals and people he had met on his trips abroad. If I could be amused by this never ending fund of stories, why would they not amuse other people? I put this idea to Gerry but he was strangely half-hearted, saying no one outside the family would want to hear these tales. I was convinced he was wrong and determined to make him see it. In the end we compromised; he agreed to write a radio talk and sent it to the BBC – at that time 15 minute talks were popular listening. Borrowing a portable typewriter from Margaret's ex-husband Jack, Gerry set to work. I prayed the talk would be accepted; not only did we need the money badly but Gerry needed a boost to his morale. No one can ever know how we and the family felt when we got the letter inviting Gerry to come up to London and record the talk. After all those wretched months of waiting on letters that never came, at last we were on our way.

It seemed as if this initial success with the radio talk unleashed a flood of creative energy from within Gerry. Soon more talks were followed by a succession of articles, all of which were eagerly accepted for publication. To me the next logical step seemed a book about his trips abroad – brother Larry had suggested this already but had urged him to write a book about each trip and not put them all in one volume. Writing a full-length book presents many problems, even to the experienced writer, so Gerry began very cautiously to sketch the outline. Then, becoming bolder, he started the first chapter. Slowly the book took shape but not before we had completely reversed our mode of living. To try to write in a house full of noisy inmates was impossible, so Gerry decided to write at night when everyone was asleep. This is not easy when you are forced to share a room with someone who is a light sleeper and who needs all of the allotted eight hours. Still, it had to be done. I think it says a great deal for our staying power that our marriage survived this final onslaught – but it is not something I would honestly recommend.

My role in life was now that of a reader, a counter of words and a corrector of spelling. I soon found that Gerry was trying to rival *War and Peace* in length; the contents were intriguing but the spelling was diabolical. As neither of us could face retyping the manuscript all corrections had to be typed on to sticky paper, cut to size and then placed over the offending word. Finally the day came and the book was sent off to Larry's publishers for their comments. They liked it and so did everyone else: critics and reading public praised it and bought it in large numbers. Gerry was overwhelmed at its success – Book Society Choice, *Daily Mail* Book Award, then the Americans and other foreign publishers bought it – it was never ending. No one was more pleased by this bonanza than brother Larry who urged Gerry quickly to write another.

This great success was not only the beginning of a completely new career for Gerry but also it enabled him to resume his animal trips. Only this time I could go with him. At the back of his mind was always the thought that, with the money he could earn from writing, he could plan for the day when he could achieve his main ambition – to have his very own zoo, but one with a difference – where animals could be kept, bred, studied and saved from extinction, thus forming a nucleus that could perhaps be reintroduced into its former wild habitat as and when circumstances permitted.

As for my own thoughts and feelings at that time; I would be untruthful if I pretended that I never regretted giving up my own career – there were times when I regretted it bitterly – but on balance I honestly believe that my decision to exchange apes for arias was right and my new way of life, in some ways, a far more rewarding one. Should the opportunity repeat itself I would do the same again. To those people, especially women involved with women's rights, who feel that a wife must necessarily always take a back seat in any marriage, I would just like to say that I certainly have not. We have been partners from the beginning, and our successes and failures have been joint ones. So far from being deprived of my own career I have shared another's, to, I hope, our mutual benefit.

Chapter Two

Big-footed Bird

When it became obvious that his first book, *The Overloaded Ark*, was going to be a great success, Gerry made plans to leave as soon as we possibly could on another collecting trip. I think as a further encouragement to me, he decided to let me make the final decision as to our destination. For some reason South America has always held a tremendous fascination for me. I do not know whether this is because, in some past incarnation, I was part of a South American civilization – I like to think so – but I was anyway determined that it was the first place I would visit. I felt a weird, almost tangible link with this magnificent continent and to be offered the chance to go there was all I could have asked for. Fortunately, Gerry was as enthusiastic about the idea as I was, and by good luck Gerry's elder brother, Larry, had made some wonderful friends and contacts when he was with the British Council in the Argentine.

Gerry also thought it would be good experience for me to find out what planning an expedition was like, so he left all the travel arrangements in my hands. I was terrified, never having done anything like this before. However, in order to prove that women were every bit as good as men at organizing, I plunged into the adventure with a wild enthusiasm which, happily for me, was rewarded by a successful trip.

On a beautiful morning in December our ship pulled alongside the tree-lined wharf in Buenos Aires. I was overwhelmed by what I saw; beautiful jacaranda trees were all over the place; bougainvillea was in bloom; it was like my idea of paradise. After struggling, with the help of the British Embassy, through the customs, we were eventually installed in a lovely flat, belonging to a friend of Larry's. She, poor woman, little realizing what she was doing, had offered us the use of the flat for as long as we wished. She herself, very wisely, had arranged to go off to the summer resort of Mar Del Plata to spend Christmas. One forgets, having lived in the Northern Hemisphere for so long, that south of the Equator the Christmas holidays are holidays in the true sense of the word, i.e. you go to the seaside.

We were blissfully happy in this flat and settled down to making plans to go out into the country and start our work. A former acquaintance of Gerry's, whom he had met in England, was a man called Ian Gibson, the son of one of the Anglo-Argentine families that had lived in that country for many generations. Fortunately for us he had great local knowledge of the fauna and flora and, which was even more important, he had relatives who owned estancias in the countryside itself. One day he came along with an invitation to go to stay at what is perhaps the oldest estancia in Argentina, called Los Ingleses, which belonged to a cousin of his.

Delighted at this prospect, we all piled into his cousin's car very early the next day and set off for the camp. Although I realized that most of the Argentine is composed of flat rolling grassland, nothing had prepared me for the fascination of sitting in that car looking at endless miles of rolling plain, punctuated only by the odd water-windmill or stand of eucalyptus trees, and bisected, at infrequent intervals, by fences, on which there seemed to be, on every single post, either a small Burrowing Owl or an Oven Bird's nest. These nests are painstakingly constructed by the thrush-like Oven Birds out of the local mud. As the Argentine mud has this lovely reddish tinge to it as well, birds and nests together look absolutely fabulous. Later we found an old and deserted nest and decided to open it. Only then could we appreciate the lovely design; it was almost like a snail shell and afforded complete protection for the bird and its offspring.

On we drove down the large concrete stretch of road. Suddenly, for no apparent reason, the cousin awoke out of a deep sleep and said, 'Ah, we turn off here'. Almost immediately we were up to our axles in glutinous mud. There had, unfortunately, been a rainstorm the night before and the Argentine mud has a very special feature; at one minute it can be a beautiful, firm, dust road but with even the slightest rainfall it turns into a quagmire. The Argentine driver coped extremely well. We soon got used to being tossed about and thrown from side to side, and so could again concentrate on the country and, what is even more breath-taking in the Argentine, the sky. This was brimming over with large, fluffy clouds of immense proportions and the most fantastic shapes – I immediately became a devoted worshipper and cloud-gazing became my most favoured occupation whilst I was in South America. Unless you have actually seen these Argentine landscapes you cannot appreciate their beauty: the combination of the greeny-brown earth, interspersed with the redness of the clay, beneath the blue and white of the sky.

Eventually, after about two hours of this thumping and banging, we came to an enormous stand of trees. Here there was an overwhelming scent of gardenias, honeysuckle and orange blossom. We drove through the huge trees which appeared like the nave of some cathedral, with branches overhanging and forming a perfect arch of shade and scented coolness, then came to this majestic white colonial house at the end. I never have been an envious person but I do really envy that family this house; it is the one property in all the world that I have ever seen that I would dearly love to own. I am happy to think that the Boote family share my feelings about the house, and love it with all the intensity of the connoisseurs they are.

Once at the house we were introduced to the rest of the family; there was Mrs Boote, her son, John, and her two daughters, Elizabeth and Rosemary. They welcomed us with that hospitality which is so important a part of the Argentine way of life. Nothing was too much trouble; everything was at our disposal. Gerry and I were shown into a large wood-panelled room, in which was a huge double bed; the mattress filled with feathers so that to sleep in it was like being submerged in an enormous goose. Outside the windows humming birds played and many other little birds came to see us. After an enormous breakfast we went out to look at the property itself. As I did not ride, I was put in a cart, while the rest went on horses. Soon we were out surveying the enormous expanse of grasslands, interspersed with lagoons, on which wildfowl of all kinds fed. As the sun by now had become really hot, it was blissful sitting there in the cart as it was dragged along lazily by the horses. Every so often we would startle a Burrowing Owl or a lapwing and around us we could hear Screamers, and the other birds that live in the pampas. I was so engrossed in soaking up this marvellous atmosphere that I did not pay much attention to the other varieties of wildlife that were obviously around. John Boote said he would organize for us a party of peons (cowboys) to help us look for any of the creatures that were to be found on his land. All too soon, we reluctantly decided that we ought to return to the house in order to eat lunch and formulate a plan of campaign.

One of the birds that we were particularly interested in getting turned out to be one of the commonest around Los Ingleses, the Crested Screamer. These are ash-grey in colour, about the size of a turkey, and wear a black band round their neck, which makes them look for all the world like reverend gentlemen. The Screamers are something of a scourge in the Argentine as they graze like geese in enormous flocks and completely devastate the fields of alfalfa in the winter. This irritating habit has caused the Argentine farmer to look upon them with a jaundiced eye and they are considered fair game for anyone with a gun. Hoots of astonishment greeted our announcement that we were interested in collecting them. 'Chahas,' said John, 'but those are pests! What on earth do you want those birds for?'

Finally we convinced them that we really did have this bizarre ambition and they cheerfully agreed to help us get some. We were particularly anxious to get hold of young birds, mainly because they would be far easier to transport than the adults, but, although we had in fact been near the area where we knew their nests must be, they were so well concealed that we had not been successful in finding any that morning. It was decided that perhaps the evening, when we were going to set up nets around the lagoons to try to catch some of the wildfowl, might be the best time for locating Screamers' nests. Sure enough, on that first evening, just as we were preparing to go back to the house, Gerry noticed a grey pile by the edge of the lagoon which on closer examination he found to be a young Screamer. He approached it gingerly, but the bird kept absolutely still. Even when he reached forward and touched its head, it did nothing. So he just picked it up, put it under his arm like a domestic fowl, and carried it back to the car.

Later, over dinner, John, still highly amused at our wanting Screamers, said to Gerry: 'You know, if you really are serious about wanting lots of those birds, I promise you that I'll get as many as you want.'

'All right,' Gerry replied, 'we'll take as many as you can get.'

'Okay,' said John, 'it's a deal.'

The following day Gerry and I were in a small hut attempting to make a few cages in readiness for all the animals that John had promised. Gerry had hit his hand twice with the hammer, and was cursing like mad when a voice shouted: 'Here are your Screamers.' This was the last straw as far as Gerry was concerned, and clutching the hammer in a belligerent way, he strode out of the hut intending to pay John out for making facetious jokes. Much to our astonishment, there indeed was John with some of his peons, all clutching bulbous bags. Open-mouthed, Gerry stared at them, and said: 'But you can't be serious. Are all those bags full of Screamers?'

'You wanted Screamers; I promised to get them for you; and being a true Argentine I've kept my promise. Have a look for yourself,' said John.

Sure enough they were Screamers, and there were eight of them. John sat and grinned, while Gerry gingerly opened each sack and peered in.

'But this is incredible. How on earth did you get them?'

John merely shrugged his shoulders, and said; 'Oh, easy. And if you want any more, you can have them tomorrow. Oh, by the way, there's a little sack here, with a youngster in it. I thought it safer to keep him separate. Would you like to have a look at him?'

Gerry was very gentle with this particular sack. Carefully he opened it up, and tipped it slightly. Inside was one of the most ridiculous and charming baby birds that we had ever seen. Gerry reckoned it could not have been much more than a week old, at most. His body was roughly the size of a coconut, absolutely circular, and at the end of a long neck was a high, domed intellectual forehead with a tiny beak and a pair of happy brown eyes. Yet it was the legs and feet which were the most outstanding features of this baby bird. They were a greyish pink in colour and had the appearance of being at least five times too big for him and not altogether under his control. To round off this bizarre appearance, he had two small, flaccid bits of skin on his back (which looked as though they had been attached there purely by accident), which were supposedly doing duty as wings. Add to this that he was entirely clad in what appeared to be a bright yellow suit of cotton wool and you have some idea of how sweet he looked.

As Gerry gently chivvied him out of the sack he fell on his back and struggled manfully on to his enormous flat feet. He stood there, raised his wings slightly and looked at us with peculiar intensity. Having decided that we were perhaps friendly, he sneepishly opened his beak and said 'Weep', then, very slowly, swayed forward, putting one foot carefully down behind the other. After this he stood stock still, evidently very pleased with himself at having accomplished so intricate a movement. This was followed by a short rest, another 'Weep', and then an attempt at another step, just to show us that he could do it more than once. The only snag was that, having taken the first step, his left foot was resting on the toes of his right. Naturally, the results were disastrous. He tried desperately to extricate his right foot but without any success. Finally, with a mighty heave, he succeeded in lifting both his feet from the ground and promptly fell flat on his face. We were all rude enough to burst into laughter, but this had no effect upon the bird except to make him give us a rather shamefaced 'Weep'.

It is a habit of ours to give any animal that we have in our care a personal name, preferably one that seems aptly to describe their character. Our original choice for the Screamer chick had been 'Egg', in recognition of his yolk-like colouring, but we never felt that this was entirely right and when he grew older and more sedate, we decided to change it slightly to 'Eggbert'.

I had never had much to do with birds until then, but Gerry assured me that he was, without doubt, one of the most funny-looking that he had ever met. He acted in such a riotous way that Gerry literally used to cry with laughter, watching him try to walk about and behave in a manner befitting a dignified Screamer.

He had a delightful habit of cocking his head on one side and saying 'Weep' whenever confronted by a situation that was not quite what he expected. He was ridiculously tame and so, every afternoon, we would take him out of his little cage for an hour's constitutional on the nearby lawn. In some ways it must have been a harrowing experience for him as his feet were a liability; not only was there so much of them but they really did seem to have a life of their own. He could never walk without tripping himself up and consequently adopted a habit of watching them very carefully, almost as though he was willing them to behave in a proper manner. One felt that the last thing he wanted was to have badly behaved feet like these and that he believed that, if he gazed at them long enough, he might cow them into submission. Having spent about ten minutes gazing intently at them, he would launch himself in an effort to rush across the lawn and perhaps, with luck, leave them behind. He tried this many times, but never quite succeeded in making a dignified exit.

Perhaps the funniest episodes we ever had with him arose when he tried desperately to catch butterflies. We had always been under the impression that Screamers were entirely vegetarian but whenever a butterfly hovered anywhere near him it was like watching a member of the fox-hunting fraternity when he hears the view-halloo; a fanatical light appeared in Eggbert's eyes and the stalking would begin. At least, we thought that was what he was up to, but unfortunately his feet did not seem to appreciate the need for stealth and cunning. Not only would he end up by treading on each toe but sometimes his feet would even try to walk in different directions. Eggbert had to concentrate hard if he were not to lose his prey, yet if he did not keep his eyes constantly on his feet, something horrible was sure to happen.

The climax to these abortive butterfly hunts came when one very forward butterfly decided that Eggbert's beak was the only possible resting place. Perhaps the creature was tired, or Eggbert may have looked like a rather inviting flower. To add insult to injury the butterfly was not content just to sit and pretend not to be there, but rudely waved its antennae round in order to draw attention to itself. Eggbert seemed deeply offended by this behaviour and threw his head back, whereupon the butterfly ascended into the air and Eggbert, in trying to make a backward swoop at it, promptly fell over on his head, feet hopelessly waving in the air. Before flying off the butterfly had the temerity to do a sort of victory roll over Eggbert's recumbent form, thus confirming once and for all his original belief that lepidoptera were never to be trusted.

Although the adult birds were relatively easy to feed on a mixture of grain and alfalfa, Eggbert himself gave us some cause for concern, because he did not seem to care for the adult mixture nor for any of the wide variety of goodies supplied by our hostess. We were becoming desperate, because we felt that such a small bird would not have large reserves of strength.

It was of paramount importance that we find something to tempt his appetite.

I think it was Elizabeth Boote who suggested that we might try releasing him into their vegetable garden at the back of the house so that he could choose his own food. Mrs Boote was sufficiently under Eggbert's spell never to have thought of saying no. With her full co-operation and blessing we launched on this exercise. It was rather like watching a miniature inspection of a guard of honour. To say that Eggbert walked down the rows of vegetables is a slight exaggeration, rather he staggered and stumbled, stopping occasionally to give a friendly peck and a 'Weep' to the odd bit of greenery. When we got to the tomatoes he did seem a little more interested, but no, having had a little taste he decided this really was not his food after all, and so he passed on, rather wearily, to the potatoes. Here there was a pause for a short nap and we all crouched down, smoked and chatted amongst ourselves, until he awoke, looking much fresher, and continued on his journey.

Carrots? Definitely not. Peas? Well perhaps, but having pottered round them for a bit, eventually, no. Then he went on to the beans. By this time, of course, we had all got rather bored by the procedure, but perked up when he seemed to be attracted to the bean flowers. Alas, this proved to be merely a passing interest, apparently more botanical than gastronomic. The mint and parsley were an equal failure, though he raised our hopes by indulging in a little bit of cleaning of the foot; perhaps an ant had got on to it or something, It ended up with Eggbert falling down once again, into a puddle, whereupon we had to pick him up, dry him and comfort him, and launch him off on the last bit of the garden, which consisted of neat rows of spinach.

Here he came to a sudden halt. We, by this time, felt rather as though we were watching a Pearl White movie or a children's Saturday afternoon serial. Every time he stopped we all froze hopefully. This time however, it really seemed as though something was going to happen. A quick peck at a leaf ended up with him tripping and falling head first into a large spinach plant. After a little while he managed to free himself and try again. He attacked an even larger leaf and found it difficult to manage, so, not to be outdone, he spread his legs, braced himself and tugged frantically. Naturally, the end of the leaf broke away and once more Eggbert was on his back, but this time clutching a tiny piece of spinach leaf in his beak. We were delighted of course. There was much cheering at Eggbert's success and eventually a large plate of chopped spinach was put before him.

Then another problem made its appearance. It was obvious that, even though we had finely chopped the leaves, the spinach was too fibrous for such a little bird. We had a conference.

'I think that we are going to have to resort to some rather spectacular method in order to feed this bird,' said Gerry.

Innocently I enquired what he had in mind.

'Well, you see, it's obvious that the mother bird would eat the greenery, and then it would be regurgitated in a fine sloppy mess.'

'I see,' I said, 'and how do you suggest that we do that?'

'Well, it's quite easy really. I suggest that one of us chews some spinach as fine as possible.'

'That's all very well,' said Elizabeth, 'but surely it would be bad for him if it were done by somebody who smoked?'

'Quite,' said Gerry.

'Well,' said Elizabeth, 'you smoke, I do, John does and so does Mother.' Slowly it dawned upon me what was about to be suggested.

'In other words, what you're all saying is that as I don't smoke, I must be the one to do it?' I asked.

'That's a jolly good idea,' said Gerry. 'Don't you all agree?'

'Yes,' they said, and added that, as I was so obviously fond of Eggbert, this was the least I could do for him. 'It's all in a good cause,' they pointed out, and made other platitudinous remarks.

So what could I do? I picked up a large plate of spinach, gave them all what I hoped was a withering look and took it off to a quiet corner. Needless to say it *did* work, and Eggbert ate quite a few platefuls of spinach during his sojourn with us. I like to think that he appreciated all that I was doing for him, but it did finally convince me that the one vegetable in the world that I could never face again was spinach.

As a complete contrast to the rather delicate feeding habits of Eggbert, we had caught a pair of Armadillos which made all our other animals' table manners seem impeccable. When we first got these large and hairy Armadillos they seemed to have no interest in anything but sleep. No amount of noise, banging, clattering, cheeping, screaming, shouting, barking seemed to have any effect upon them, they would just lie smugly in their box. They were two females who seemed devoted to one another.

It was quite by accident that we discovered their true characters. The first evening we filled a tin tray high with the mixture that apparently Armadillos like and put it in the outside portion of the cage. We were not quite sure how they would respond to this food, which by the way consisted of a mixture of chopped meat, offal, raw egg and fruits, all mixed together with milk. It looked offputting, but was obviously ambrosia as far as Armadillos were concerned. Without warning these two slumbering lumps erupted like a volcano. They hit the tin amidships, and they and the tin ended up in the far corner in a tangled heap, submerged in a wave of food. They then spent the next half hour chasing bits of this glutinous mess round the cage and sucking them off each other. You would never have believed that it was possible for two animals to get through such a lot of food, particularly when it was stuck to every part of their anatomy and to the structure of the cage itself, yet within less than half an hour there was not any area that had been overlooked. Contented, they retired to their bedroom to lie on their backs and snore gently.

Eggbert always watched the feeding habits of his hut companions with a great deal of interest and obvious disdain. After all, he was of a far more delicate nature and so, one assumed, he rather despised this unmannerly display of greed.

It was with great sadness that I saw our animals off at Buenos Aires Airport. It was not possible to hold on to them as we were on our way to Paraguay, and so, reluctantly, it was decided that the best thing to do was to send Eggbert, the two (and by this time very fat) Armadillos and other specimens that we had collected so far, back to England. Although we did eventually catch many more Screamers and Armadillos none of them had the charm of Eggbert, nor the eating capacity of the terrible twins.

Chapter Three

Nicotine and Night Monkeys

It was entirely due to Bebita Ferreyra that we eventually ended up in Paraguay. She, like most Argentines, seemed to have friends everywhere – including one who owned a large tanning estate, called Puerto Casado, up on the Brazilian–Bolivian border.

In order to get to this remote area it was necessary first to fly on a regular flight to Asunción, the capital of Paraguay and then to get the company's private single-engine plane to take us to the estate itself. So it was very early one beautiful morning that we made our way to a small airfield just outside Asunción where we hopefully expected to get into the small plane. Whilst we were waiting, stretching and yawning, the pilot approached us, smiling broadly, and started to pick up all our luggage. This, much to everyone's surprise, including the pilot's, just fitted into the plane, only leaving enough room for us to squeeze in beside him.

We had never had this sort of experience before, and, as at that time flying held no terrors for us, it was with tremendous interest that we looked forward to this two-hour flight over the fringes of the notorious Matto Grosso. It was a unique opportunity to see the various types of country which make up Paraguay. The river Paraguay itself acted as a sort of break between the two kinds of country which passed below us. On one hand was the rich red earth and the green forest, which made up the eastern part of Paraguay; on the other bank of the river spread the Chaco, which appeared, from the height that we were flying, to be a level plain which stretched endlessly to the horizon. Even at this height it looked still and devoid of life of any kind. What was most obvious was that it was waterlogged and indeed, was really marsh land rather than the dry grass plain which we had been used to in the Argentine. Instead of the eucalyptus or poplars that we had seen further south, there were clumps of palm trees. It was peculiar country and, by comparison with the pampas, monotonous to look at. The main thought that passed through my mind was that, should we have the misfortune to crash in this particular type of country, we would probably either drown or, even worse, be lost forever. An additional attraction would be the charming livestock of every type and kind that inhabits swampy marshland, such as leeches and mosquitoes.

Eventually, after what seemed like hours, the pilot shouted, 'Puerto Casado,' pointing below. The plane started to descend. The first thing that hit us both as the door of the plane opened was the heat; it rushed in with the force of a tornado and used as Gerry was to the hot humidity of West Africa even he was almost bowled over by its sudden impact.

We hastily got out of the plane and loaded our bags on to the truck, which had appeared alongside. This was to take us to the nearby village where the company had put a house at our disposal for the duration of our stay. We were eagerly looking forward to the couple of months that we would be there as we had been assured, by everyone who knew Paraguay, that it was teeming with animal life, particularly the sort of things that we were looking for.

As we ate a rather late breakfast at the company house, the pilot tried out his halting English and we our few words of Spanish. One thing that did come out clearly and unmistakably, when he finally took his departure, was his surprise that I should be in the Chaco at all. He paused in the doorway, gave me a beaming smile and said: 'Are you sure you won't change your mind and come back to Asunción with me now?'

Naturally, this question took me by surprise, so I enquired why he should think that, having only just arrived, I might now want to go back?

'Well, when you've seen the size of our mosquitoes and have tried to get through all this water,' he waved his hands expansively to encompass, presumably, the whole of the Chaco, 'I feel sure this is the last place you'll want to stay.'

Summoning all the feminine courage I could, I gave him what I hoped was a scornful glare and assured him that the last thing I would ever contemplate was leaving Puerto Casado before our work was done.

'*Bueno*,' he said, bowing slightly from the waist, 'I will see you next week, I think,' and laughing, went out of the door. I would never have dreamed of telling him how right he really was, but within the next two days I would have given almost anything to be anywhere but in Puerto Casado.

Normally the natives of a country tend to exaggerate the drawbacks in the hope of frightening off the tourist, as any visitor to a country is always regarded. Even in Australia, a country I love very much indeed and whose people I like equally, they still indulge in this rather childlike practice of trying to frighten off the would-be visitor who intends to, say, cross the desert in a car, or drive on unmade roads, by assuring you that they are, without doubt, the worst that anyone has ever come across anywhere in the world. Yet I was soon to learn that our pilot had been, indeed, extremely truthful and obviously had far more sense than I had – the mosquitoes were the largest and most abundant either of us had ever encountered and the climate did nothing to make up for the horrors of the local insects.

The next couple of days were completely taken up with establishing a sort of base area. There was an abandoned chicken run behind the company house where it was agreed it would be safest to keep any animals that we collected. It consisted of a sheltered area, complete with roof, and a large wired-in space which had been especially protected to keep out possible predators. It was suggested it would be safer to keep any animals behind this wire just in case the odd fox or snake was tempted to invade the camp. This time, we did heed the local advice because we felt that they knew far more about their predators' habits than we did. The enclosure had not been used for quite a long time and so it was necessary to give it a thorough cleaning. With the help of one of the little Indian boys, we set to and within a couple of days it was looking reasonably spruce. In the meantime, the manager and his staff sent messages out along the narrow gauge railway line, which served to link the main area and village with the outlying tree-felling camps.

This railway was a charming contraption consisting of open cars and flat cars, pulled by an ancient V8 Ford engine mounted on railway wheels. Apparently, this had been running for quite a time and was an extremely reliable way to transport people and goods, as well as trees, from deep in the Chaco. Through careful engineering they managed to ensure that the track itself did not become submerged by the surrounding marshland, even when there was a heavy downpour.

Puerto Casado itself actually bordered on the river Paraguay and so it was a perfect centre for sending messages in all directions, by river, by rail, or even by the odd horseman who braved the swamps to get into the village. As at Los Ingleses we first concentrated on cage building in readiness for all the creatures we felt confident would appear, fortunately helped by a local man who had far more experience of carpentry than either Gerry or myself, although I will say that both of us are rather a dab hand at creating a temporary cage.

I personally had greatly looked forward to establishing a base camp as it was an entirely new experience for me and I was anxious to impress my dear husband with my abilities. He had assured me on previous occasions that I was a quick and adept student, so I was really determined to show him that I was already a fully-fledged animal keeper. I looked forward eagerly to receiving my first charge.

In any animal collection as in any group of humans one often gets the odd outstanding character. As I was to learn during the years I spent handling animals, there is no logical explanation why one individual creature should display so tremendous a personality and yet it happens again and again. It was in Paraguay that I encountered my very first.

We were having a leisurely lunch one day cooked by Paula, our Indian housekeeper, whose main occupation as madame of the local brothel conferred a lot of side benefits, such as a constant supply of house-cleaners and laundresses. Also it meant that if there were any special foods going, (and this was particularly important when keeping animals), Paula knew just how to get them. She probably browbeat the local market keepers by threatening to cut off their entertainment, or some other similar form of blackmail. We were savouring some special concoction of hers when she suddenly appeared at the dining-room door, followed by a very old-looking Indian. Paula (with obvious reluctance) decided to act as intermediary between the Indian, who only spoke the local language of Guarani, and ourselves, whom she was convinced spoke fluent Spanish.

Trailing behind the Indian at the end of a lead was a monkey, but a monkey with a difference and one I certainly had never seen before. With obvious delight, Gerry leapt to his feet and advanced upon the visitor, who by this time was getting a bit worried, having been confronted first by a disapproving Paula and now by a rather large and excited European. The monkey was, as Gerry later explained, a Douracouli, which is the only nocturnal monkey in the world. There are, apparently, two distinct species and it is strange that they also have very distinctive personalities. Later we realized that we had been lucky in picking the nicer variety of the two.

As the local name for Douracoulis is Cai Poucarais, we decided immediately to call the new arrival Cai. She was about the size of the average domestic cat and her fur was basically grey, but with the overtones of silver that tree lichen has. The chest fur was a rather pale orange which became lighter as it progressed down her tummy. The ears seemed almost non-existent, being so deeply buried in the hair, but it was the eyes that were riveting; they were enormous and owl-like, a beautiful pale amber colour, edged with white fur tipped in black. In fact, the whole aspect of the face was owl-like, but the thing that struck me most was that the mouth was shaped into a permanent smile. Thus the whole aspect of the animal was one of great warmth, friendliness and almost understanding.

The man, apparently, had been keeping the monkey at his home – it being a local tradition to keep animals as pets and then, eventually, to use them for food. This may sound callous to people like ourselves, who do not lack animal protein, but when one remembers that native populations are totally dependent upon the wild creatures as their source of protein, it becomes understandable, if not attractive. We have benefited greatly by the practice since many of the animals that have come into our possession over the years have only been preserved by the protection of people who destined them eventually for the cooking pot. Of course, the locals think that anyone who pays good hard cash for what, after all, is a wild animal, must be an idiot and therefore is to be swindled as quickly as possible before sense dawns. When you think about it, this is a perfectly logical attitude for them to take, because they cannot possibly appreciate our deep interest in their native fauna. They regard wild creatures as we do our cattle and sheep, a source of food and little else.

Poor Cai was in a very tattered state and was naturally apprehensive and nervous, for her experience with humans, so far, had obviously not been exactly happy. We made no attempt to make friendly overtures to her; feeling that, by giving her food and leaving her alone, she might perhaps get over her insecurity and look upon us with more tolerance. She loved everything we gave her but, however much the food tempted her, always waited until we had gone away before coming out of her little box in order to get at it.

Gerry was anxious, as I was, that she should be given a lot of food and, what is even more important, as much variety as possible, so when a little native boy brought in some half-dead lizards, Gerry decided to kill one and offer it to her. Her behaviour at being confronted by this new source of food was amazing – gone immediately was her caution, she leapt out of her box, gave a weird, faint scream and grabbed the lizard out of Gerry's hand. For a minute it looked as though she had suddenly remembered that we were nearby and that she must retreat, but then all caution was thrown to the wind as the reptile in her hand twitched and her attention was again riveted to it. This prompted her to set to and dispatch it with obvious delight, rather like a child eating a bar of barley sugar. We stood perfectly still until the last morsel had disappeared. To make sure that no little bits had escaped her notice, she did the usual monkey thing of examining her hands minutely. The surrounding area of ground was then inspected, just in case any bits had dropped. Having satisfied herself that not one scrap had been overlooked she gave herself a shake, a little scratch and with a shrug of what one might call perhaps contempt, returned to her box. From that day, she overcame any fright she ever had with us and accepted our attentions willingly.

At first we kept Cai on a long leash, as she had been used to this, but after a few days we noticed that she preferred to spend more and more time (when not eating, of course) in the box that she used as a sleeping area. Gerry decided the time had come to build her a tall cage with a special sleeping area attached to it. When we eventually moved, she would have to spend the three-week sea voyage in this cage.

Cai took to it at once, particularly the bedroom, which had a door to it which we left open so that she could have the odd look around whenever she felt inclined. It is a strange thing that all South American creatures have enormous curiosity. They love to know what is going on around them and, I think, in a way, this adds greatly to their confidence in their dealings with you. It certainly worked that way for Cai. She trusted us to the extent even of sleeping with the door open; a great compliment from an animal who is obviously nervous and, by instinct and training, must be always alert for a possible enemy.

She would spend most of the day snoozing gently, but should anything interesting happen or there be an unusual noise, her eyes would open immediately and she would peep round the bedroom door to investigate, twisting her head just like an owl or a cat to get the best view she could. Like a child, she had to see everything that went on. Even when it was obvious that she was frightened (as she always was at the sight of snakes) nothing stopped her persistent interest in all the camp activities.

On one occasion, Gerry brought in some rotten logs for one of our woodpeckers to play with and chopped a little off them to get them into the cage. In doing so, he came across some large, gorgeous-looking cockroaches.

'This will make a marvellous tit-bit for Cai,' said Gerry, waving one of these nauseous creatures at me. 'Shall I give it to her, or will you?'

I declined, for I cannot overcome my revulsion at cockroaches, especially ones of those dimensions. So, with my full permission, he carried it over to her.

At this precise juncture she was spread-eagled on the floor of the cage, rather like a sun-bather on a beach, with closed eyes and mouth sagging open. When Gerry called her name she woke up immediately and looked at him in an astonished fashion. Opening the door of the cage he inserted the largest of the cockroaches. Her reaction was startling; what we thought would be an amusing tit-bit for her must have seemed like a charging rhino or something similar, for she shot from the floor of her cage right up to the branch nearest her bedroom opening, obviously trying to get as far away from the cockroach as she possibly could. In the meantime, the cockroach merely sat there waving its antennae about. Cai retreated even further into the bedroom, turned round and poked her head cautiously out of the opening to watch the intruder with obvious suspicion and foreboding. After a little while she apparently convinced herself that it was not quite so terrifying, and might even be edible. She decided to come down the branch a little and have a closer look. The cockroach was completely unconcerned by this activity and settled down to cleaning its antennae.

Cai sat and contemplated it, her hands folded over her tummy. Then, cautiously but delicately, she tapped the back of the cockroach with a trembling finger. The poor insect scuttled off across the floor whilst Cai leapt backwards in such consternation that she nearly fell off the branch. The cockroach meanwhile had reached the front of the cage and started to squeeze through the wire. It must have dawned upon Cai that perhaps it was really food after all and that she was about to lose it. She made a quick grab to prevent it from getting away but was unfortunately too late. Luckily Gerry was there to retrieve the cockroach and push it back in. This time the silly animal followed the cockroach about, tapping it with her fingers which she then smelt. This went on for some time until, finally, she made up her mind that she must try to eat it. Screwing up her face with obvious distaste, she grabbed the cockroach with both hands and stuffed it into her mouth, leaving the hind legs outside, wiggling frantically. She obviously enjoyed it once it had finally gone down, but we were left to conclude that, as she was a monkey of little courage and enterprise, it might be a good idea to save her having a heart attack or something similar if we killed any other insects that might be around before we gave them to her.

After this, Cai became tame and totally trusted us both. I loved her dearly. Although I realize that collecting animals is not a matter of clutching cuddly fluffy creatures to your bosom, it is nevertheless very pleasant from time to time to have a fluffy cuddly creature that you can do this with. I never attempted to pick her up but she would allow me to stroke her and play with her and we had lovely games together. In one of her favourites I would hold a piece of banana or a grape in my clenched hand. Cai would come down from her bedroom and solemnly open my hand, finger by finger, until she could get at the hidden fruit.

It was a tremendous fillip to us to see the great improvement in her condition which plenty of fruit, milk, raw eggs and vitamins, plus the odd insect, had achieved. She put on weight quickly and soon became a glossy Douracouli with a fur as dense as a sheep's. One honestly could not have believed it was the same animal as had been presented to us that lunch-time; she was worth all the effort that I, particularly, had put into gaining her confidence. I began to dread the day when I would have to hand her over to someone else, for she had become very dear to me. In a way, gaining her trust and confidence had been a humbling experience. I honestly think it was from my association with Cai that I learned to appreciate the tremendous privilege it was to be allowed to look after and protect wild creatures.

Another outstanding 'character' was a Crab-eating Raccoon whom we decided to call 'Pooh' for a variety of reasons; the most obvious one I am sure I need not explain. Although he was not a bear, he did have some of the more endearing characteristics of Winnie-the-Pooh. An Indian hunter brought him to us. At the beginning he resembled a Chow puppy, with fluffy black and white ringed tail and a mask of black fur across the eyes which made him look like a comic burglar; out of this peered two lugubrious brown eyes. Raccoons have immensely large, flat feet, the soles of which are bright pink, but this is redeemed by fingers and toes of long, artistic proportions.

We put him into a very roomy cage. To begin with he behaved as a model visitor, sitting on his fat backside and gazing at us through the slats of the cage, looking, Gerry said, like a highwayman awaiting trial. It soon became apparent, however, that we should not be taken in by the air of innocence which emanated from him.

The lock on the cage we thought quite secure and so we went off to lunch quite happily. However, when we returned it was to find him surrounded by what was left of our day's egg supply and covered with a mixture of yolk and white. When we scolded him, he gazed at us with the expression of a person who had led a deprived and unappreciated childhood; he was obviously deeply hurt by our unreasonably strong reaction to his escapade. For the life of us, we could not understand how he had managed to get out of the cage in the first place, so, we decided to hide and watch in case he tried to do it again.

To begin with nothing happened. Then a black snout whiffled between the bars, trying to decide whether we had gone. Having come to the conclusion that the coast was clear, long slender fingers groped in the direction of the catch on the door. Eventually, having found it, one of the fingers was gently pushed under the hook and, with an expertise which would have pleased any burglar, the latch was disengaged, the door pushed open and a very pleased face appeared around it. We just reached the food table in time.

Eventually, his cage began to resemble something that would have baffled Houdini, but no matter what we devised, he would eventually find a way of opening it. Soon it became a bigger bind for us to open the doors in order to clean and feed him than it was for him to get out. Strangely, he never tried to escape but merely went straight for the food stores, not because he wanted to eat them but to demolish them in order to make a kind of monster omelette and to cover himself with as much of the sticky mess as possible. Deprived he was not; in fact, we reckoned that he cost us more to feed than any other animal we ever had or were ever likely to have in the collection. It was a compulsive sense of destruction that inhabited him.

In desperation we bought a huge padlock. Even with this on the door, he was not convinced escape was impossible. Every day he would devote at least the first half-hour to playing with the padlock in the fond hope that, by patting it and jiggling it up and down, a miracle would happen and it would suddenly spring open.

Having concluded that escape was not to be, he would turn his attention to helping us clean his cage. Every day we would take out the wet sawdust and put in a fresh pile. To begin with we would spread the layer as carefully as possible over the entire cage bottom, whereupon Pooh would suddenly decide that this was not what he wanted at all. Then the sweeping began. Dog-like, using his front paws, he would shoot the sawdust through his back legs, so that it would eventually end up in a pile in one corner of the cage. Being a lover of comfort he felt a pile of sawdust to loll against was essential. The only solution was to provide him with enough both for lolling and to act as a general absorbent. In the end he would get rather bored with reclining against his mound of sawdust and took to lying on it, on his back, plucking at his stomach hair and patting his growing pot in a reflective manner. Finally, putting a hind foot in his mouth, he would gently rock himself to sleep.

His growing girth and food consumption made us feel he needed exercise, so Gerry thought it would be a good idea to put him on a lead for a few hours every day, attached to a stake which we had driven well into the ground. It was easy to make him a collar out of plaited string and a lead out of rope, but within half an hour he had gnawed his way through this, visited the food table, and devoured most of our banana supply for the day, plus the other odd tit-bits he could get his hands on. A piece of chain did restrict his activities slightly, but he got easily bored. In order to exercise his intellect, we gave him odd things to play with; pieces of wood, the odd corn husk and, when we began to film the various animals in the collection, a piece of cine film. This last item kept him thoroughly amused for days on end. He would roll it around him, wrap it round his neck, tie it round his legs and have a generally fabulous time, giving all the appearance of a film tycoon cutting his latest Biblical epic.

By this device we managed to amuse and occupy our restless spirit, at least for a few days, but in the end the novelty wore off and the film became tattered. Quite by accident one day a coconut rolled in his direction. At first he was reluctant to go near this strange thing but finally, overcoming his suspicion, he shuffled sideways towards it, ready to run away instantly if he was attacked. After touching it gingerly with one delicate paw and discovering that it would neither attack nor run away, but just roll, he got very excited and spent the next hour pursuing it round and round until it rolled beyond the limit of his chain. Piercing screams made us willing retrievers. I suggested that we bore a hole in the husk, just to see what he would do with it. This was a great success as he spent days with the nut clasped firmly between his hind paws, poking his hands down into the hole, occasionally retrieving the odd piece of inside and chewing it reflectively. It became almost an extension of him, for not only did he play with it all day but he used to fall asleep with it clutched to him like a Teddy bear. Naturally, we made sure that in future we had a constant supply of coconuts in order to preserve the sanctity of our food table.

The next addition was a small grey Pampas Fox, whom we called, not very originally I regret to say, Foxy. He again had been found by an Indian and kept as a pet. When he came to us he could not have been more than about three months old. These little foxes are charming and not only look like dogs, being the size of a terrier, but behave very like them. Foxy certainly displayed none of the more unpleasant characteristics of the fox family. Neat and slender in build, he had a most ingratiating grin and, when anything obviously pleased him, would fold back his top lip and show his teeth in the most idiotic manner. Here again, we decided to keep him on a lead rather than put him into a cage, for he was perfectly tame and friendly. We used the old-fashioned method of a ring threaded on a wire stretched between two posts, for in this way, he would get a tremendous amount of exercise and have a large area to roam in. At night we kept him in a box which we filled with dried grass.

Every morning, when released from the box, he would greet us with delight, leaping, bounding, and wagging his tail. We had to be careful how we held him, because he was so overcome with seeing us again after all that dreadful length of time that he could not really contain himself, and we were quite likely to be inundated by a deluge of saliva at one end and steaming urine at the other. His two passions in life, we soon discovered, were chickens and cigarette butts. The former addiction was quite natural, of course, in a fox or indeed in a dog. If, as happened on several occasions, one or two of Paula's fowls happened to come by our enclosure, he would crouch down ready to pounce on them, ears back and tail swishing from side to side. The stupid hens, of course, did not realise that a possible enemy was close by and often came too close, whereupon he would leap at them and send them scurrying hysterically back to where they should rightfully be. He was obviously amused by all this uproar because he would turn round, look at us, and give us one of his fatuous grins.

The cigarette butt addiction was more worrying. I did not smoke but Gerry and all the Indians did and were apt to dispose of their cigarette ends wherever they happened to be when they stopped smoking. Not thinking that an animal would crave cigarette butts, they took no precautions to keep them away from Foxy. On finding the butts Foxy would devour them with great eagerness but also with a weird expression of distaste on his face. Then would follow what could only have been a most uncomfortable half-hour of violent coughing, at the end of which he would have a very long drink of his water and be ready for any other butt that might come his way.

Nothing we could do could break the habit until, on one dreadful day, Nemesis struck. Carelessly Gerry, who was making an intricate bird cage, put down his cigarettes, not realizing that Foxy could quite easily get at them. Before we could do anything, Foxy had indeed not only found them but had polished off the whole packet. I think by this time Foxy's poor stomach had decided that it really must do something drastic to prevent this constant invasion of tobacco, and so it reacted with appalling violence. Seemingly every single shred of tobacco was regurgitated, as indeed was everything else that Foxy had eaten that day. The poor animal was so weak and exhausted by this eruption that even chickens could walk right past him without the slightest twitch of his nose. We starved him for the rest of that day but relented sufficiently by the evening to offer him a bit of meat and two raw eggs. Then, by way of an experiment, Gerry offered his cigarette packet to Foxy. The cure had been dramatically effective; he backed away hurriedly, sneezing madly. Never again was Foxy tempted by the dreaded weed.

Chapter Four

Bullets and Bichos

One of the most ridiculous birds I have ever met is the Guira Cuckoo. This spreads from the northern part of Paraguay down to the plains of the Argentine. When we were staying at Los Ingleses outside Buenos Aires, we had seen several flocks of them flying around but, to our regret, had never caught any.

One day, when we were walking along the railway line at Puerto Casado, we were suddenly confronted by a small group of them sitting on the ground. As we got nearer they made no attempt to fly away and so Gerry said: 'They're obviously waiting for us to pick them up, so come along, let's do it.' Amazingly, they continued to sit tight in spite of this threat and our continued approach. In the end we managed to catch some and our Indian guide also collected a couple.

They are about the size of the European starling but that is where the resemblance ends, because the cuckoos are a pale fawny-cream in colour, which is streaked with a weird greenish-black. They have a tatty crest on their heads and long magpie-like tails. In many ways they are bizarre creatures. Not only are they totally devoid of fear (as witnessed by the ease with which we caught them) but, once taken, they carry on as though they were born to captivity. They make no fuss about being put into cages, they do not flap and beat around or get worried; in fact they are everything an animal collector could want a specimen to be.

From the beginning, they exhibited no fear of us; on the contrary, whenever we appeared, a wild light came into their ginger eyes, their tatty crests were immediately erected and they proceeded to give us a whirring greeting. They were the most engaging creatures and endeared themselves to everyone who came into contact with them. They thought nothing of leaping out on to our heads or shoulders and would sit there quite unconcernedly, never making any attempt to fly away. It really was extraordinary to get this behaviour in a wild bird. I remember one day, Gerry was severely startled when one of them took a piece of his hair in his beak and pulled at it ferociously, I think in the fond hope that it was something edible.

I remember now that Ian Gibson had told us that they were naturally tame and had no fear at all when they were young. When they get to be fully adult, they are not quite so trusting, which is probably a good thing since otherwise they would not manage to survive so well, with the average local person being only interested in collecting animals for food. When we first got them we put them into one of our cages and they carried on as though they were long-lost friends, meeting again after many, many years of separation. Raising their crests they gazed lovingly into each other's eyes and then trilled excitedly at one another.

Though at first I thought these birds lacked charm and character, I soon found that every day I became more and more attached to them. When they had been with us only a few hours, I remember, I inserted a finger through the wire and waggled it in the direction of one of the birds. Without hesitation he rushed up to the bars and presented his head, obviously expecting to be scratched. The others were not to be outdone either, and so they all rushed down in the hope that I had enough fingers to go round. In the end they were almost like a bird pyramid, perched one on top of another. As the scratching went on, they stretched up their necks, their crests came up and their heads were raised until their beaks pointed skywards with their eyes closed in ecstasy. Quite definitely mental, Gerry pronounced, and I had to agree with him, especially when the top cuckoo, being carried away more than the others, actually overbalanced and fell down to the bottom of the cage. He merely shook himself and started to climb up again. All the many pairs of cuckoos we obtained were as daft as the first ones. I do not know what it is about the cuckoo make-up, but they are the only birds that we have ever come across that so readily accept humans and the whole idea of captivity.

Their stupidity was not total for, as we were to find out later, they did have amazing powers of recognition.

In addition they had a tremendous curiosity. This afforded us endless amusement, for we had put them in a cage with a large slot at the bottom. This enabled us to push things in without opening the doors, and to clean out any mess that they had made. For the cuckoos it could not have been better arranged. They spent almost all the time when they were not eating, chirruping or snoozing, squatting on the floor with their heads sticking out of this gap so that they could keep a close watch on everything that went on in the camp.

On top of this, they had a passion for sun-bathing. The slightest ray of sunshine in their cage caused them to go berserk and to crowd on to a perch in a large heap so as to prepare themselves for the pleasure to come. They obviously viewed sun-bathing with all the seriousness of a human sun-worshipper and, exactly as with the human, the position and the posture were of vital importance. They balanced skilfully on their perches so that, even if they became comatose and forgot actually to grip the bar, they would not necessarily fall off. All the feathers were then shaken vigorously, the tail feathers lowered, eyes closed, and the head would droop on to the breast-bones, resting against the perch so that you would have breast feathers dangling on one side and tail dangling on the other. Like this they would sit swaying very, very delicately, looking like feather dusters and, as Gerry cruelly pointed out, moth-eaten ones as well.

So these creatures would pass blissful days: greeting

us with loud shrieks of joy, gazing out of the slot at the bottom of their cage or sun-bathing in a stupor. They were without doubt the happiest birds that I ever encountered.

On our return to England, having no place of our own, we handed them over to London Zoo and so did not see them again for some considerable time. Imagine our surprise when we went into the Bird Room and approached their cage, some three months later, to have them recognize us. They rushed over to the end of their perch, glared at us with their mad eyes, erected their crests and chirruped wildly. To make sure we were not mistaken, we went back two or three times. Each time exactly the same thing happened. Checking with the bird keeper, he confirmed that they did not do this with anyone else. I think this proves that at least one section of our collection remembered and approved of us.

Originally, we had decided, before coming to Paraguay, that the easiest way of getting our collection back to the coast would be to bring it by river boat. This seemed to pose no problems, as Puerto Casado was in fact slap on the river Paraguay itself. However, we reckoned without the human element; a thing that one always hopes to avoid when going on a collecting trip but never does. About a week before we were due to leave, Paula suddenly appeared early one morning, clutching our tray of tea and jabbering in a flood of incoherent Spanish. When we eventually got her to calm down and speak more slowly, we at last understood that the favourite sport of South America had erupted in Asunción, namely, a revolution. We treated this news with great mirth because, we argued, after football, revolution is the only thing South Americans seem to enjoy. Was not one lot of revolutionaries pretty much like another?

On our way to breakfast Gerry decided that he would call in at the radio station, where we soon realized how serious everything really was. From what the operator could gather, the rebels had commandeered all the river shipping. Since then he had had no further news. We made our way back to the house soberly and very despondent, but when we reported the news to Paula she merely laughed. 'There you are, you see. I told you the last one we had lasted six months,' she said cheerfully. Trying not to look too shattered at the thought of having to stay in Puerto Casado for a further six months, we tried to explain that we had to get back to Buenos Aires because we had a ship to catch and there were people waiting for us. What was even more important was that we would by that time have certainly run out of funds and wouldn't even be able to pay her bills.

'Oh, that doesn't matter, we don't worry about money up here,' she said.

A lot of schemes flooded into our heads, wild ideas like going over into Brazil and many other impossible solutions to an equally impossible situation. Then a friendly American neighbour came to our rescue. We had met him some time before on his way through to his own property further up the river. It was a habit in South America to drop in on your neighbour on the way to or from the capital, not only to be friendly but in case they needed anything vital and he had stopped off to pay his respects and see what was going on.

After some difficulty we ran this man to earth by radio and explained our predicament.

'I'd love to help you,' he said, 'but it seems to me that whatever happens you're going to be forced to leave all your animals behind.'

Gerry naturally did not like this idea but, as the American went on to explain, his own plane, which he would willingly lend us, was hardly big enough to take us, let alone our animals as well.

We prayed that there would be a parley. Apparently this often happened in South American revolutions and, if there appeared to be a genuine truce during which negotiations took place, the international operators would put their planes down, however briefly, in the capital in order to take out those non-Paraguayans who wished to leave the country.

In the meantime we indulged in a tremendous amount of heart searching. After you have spent a considerable number of weeks looking after creatures then, however much you try, they become an integral part of your life. Still worse, there are, of course, always certain creatures to which you cannot prevent yourself becoming too closely attached. This is always fatal, especially for people like us, who know that their life is such that they will eventually have to pass most of them on to someone else. Gerry and I looked calculatingly and, we hoped, rationally at our position and after a great deal of debate decided to abandon as much of our equipment as possible. Gerry himself decided to make little cages out of lightweight wire netting, that would transport the one or two animals that we obviously had to take with us. Once in Buenos Aires we felt sure that all our friends, led by Bebita Ferreyra, would rush immediately to our aid. So we started sadly to disband the collection.

'Remember our American friend said we had to let them *all* go,' said Gerry.

'But we simply can't,' I protested. 'We *can't* let them all go. Some of them wouldn't last two minutes in the wild. We'll have to take with us at least the babies and the ones which have got too tame, even if it means leaving everything else behind.'

'All right, have it your own way. But which ones do we keep?' asked Gerry.

At that time we had on our hands an endearing but helpless baby Giant Anteater called Sarah. She was devoted to Gerry and without him simply would not have survived for more than a few minutes in the wild state, for these little creatures spend most of their early infancy clinging to their mothers' backs and are totally dependent on them for support. Obviously, she would have to come with us. Equally, I could not bear the thought of leaving Cai, the Doura-couli, behind and then there was Pooh, who by this time had become a more sensible member of the community.

'Well, and then there are the Orange Armadillos,' said Gerry. 'They're far too rare to leave. Also the Horned Toads.'

'What about my cuckoos?' I asked.

'Look, you know,' said Gerry hopelessly, 'if we go on like this, we're not going to be able to get anything away, not even ourselves. There's only a limited amount of room on that plane and we've got to be sensible.'

'I assume that in a small plane of this kind weight is the most important factor?'

'Yes,' said Gerry.

'Well, let's try and borrow a pair of scales from somebody. First of all we weigh the essential things that we've got to take with us, like your cine camera and the film and the recording machine and some of our personal stuff. We know how much we weigh ourselves and we can assume the pilot will weigh about the same as you. Let's fix a rigid limit for the total weight, work out how much is left over and then we can see how many animals we can fit in.'

'OK,' said Gerry, 'that sounds sensible. Sarah can travel on my lap, so we don't have to worry too much about her.'

'Well, I can have the recording machine and the cine camera on my lap, so in fact most of the luggage area can be filled with our suitcase and the animals. I seem to remember that the plane was about the size of the one that we flew up from Asunción in. If that's so, we've got the spare passenger seat, plus the baggage compartment.'

Buoyed up by this thought, we embarked upon an exercise which I, personally, hope never to have to indulge in again. Naturally, we put off liberation day for as long as possible, but we were finally forced into a decision when we heard that early the next morning our friendly American's plane would be flying in. He apparently, had heard that there was to be a parley, and had arranged with the Asunción office of the airline that we would be booked space on the first available flight out to Buenos Aires, together with our animals.

The birds were fairly easy to release. A Tiger Bittern whom we had patched up, having found him in a swamp with a broken wing, seemed quite happy to potter off again into the reeds. This was also the case with the various ibises that we collected, although one did seem rather desolate at the thought of being left to fend for himself again. It was the parrots and parakeets that were the worst. They had, throughout, been on a fairly friendly footing with us. They had slept in their boxes but spent all day up a tree so were perfectly at liberty to go at any time they felt inclined. They had become used to us and to being fed, and did not see why they should be expected to give up all this to return to the doubtful pleasures of freedom. Indeed, they were still sitting disconsolately in the tree near the enclosure when we left the camping site the next day.

The armadillos were easy. They simply scampered off after being released. I suppose it made no difference to them whether they were in a box or left in a clump of grass.

It was still a gloomy day, however. It was pathetic to see the parrots and some of the small birds looking wistfully at us. We had decided that we would not feed them that day because, as Gerry said: 'They'll never learn to fend for themselves and they've got to realize that they must go.'

Thanks to Paula we had managed to persuade the local inhabitants to allow all our animals to make their way back into the Chaco without being molested – I think that Paula was sufficiently dominant in that area to have her orders obeyed. Foxy, in particular, was very worried by all the activity. He was to be left with Paula who, I think, adored him as much as we did, with the assurance that, if he became unhappy, he would be released.

Perhaps the most interesting moment was when we let the snakes go. By this time we had an excellent collection, ranging from rattlesnakes to coral snakes and the most beautiful anacondas, including an extremely rare ten foot long Southern Anaconda who had become very tame since we caught him. This anaconda was particularly reluctant to leave us. We took him back to the same lake as we had caught him in and Gerry undid the neck of the sack and gently tipped him out on to the grass. The snake just lay there and refused to move, whatever noise we made. Finally, Gerry had to go up to him, grab him by the head, gather the folds up as closely as possible and then walk out into the lake and throw the anaconda as far as he could towards the middle. The interesting thing was that, although the creature must have realized that he was now completely free, he merely swam up and down and round in circles, looking at us all the time; unusual behaviour for a snake who normally slides off at the first available opportunity. It certainly confirmed our opinion about anacondas in general; that they are much maligned creatures and only attack when really provoked.

Needless to say it was dear old Pooh, the raccoon, who gave us the most trouble. His attitude was understandable. He had had a tremendous amount of freedom and he could not now see why we wanted him to go into a small wire cage. Nothing we could do would induce him to go in of his own accord, so, thoroughly exasperated, Gerry grabbed him and forced him through the door. This indignity was soon forgotten, for finding an egg inside he grabbed it between his two front paws and sucked it in a pensive way. Thereafter he ceased to be any trouble, at least until we got to Buenos Aires.

I do not think Gerry or I slept at all that night; we could not get over the emotional wrench of saying goodbye to all our creatures and we prayed they would all by now have gone from around the compound.

Alas, this was not to be. The parrots and other birds were still sitting in the tree squawking and screaming, flying past at intervals in an effort to coax us to give them some food, while one or two of the other creatures we could hear nearby.

'You know,' said Gerry, 'I think this is a perfect example of how unsatisfactory human relations with animals usually are. Most people go on about captivity being cruel and the animals loathing it and so on. Perhaps to a certain extent, some of them do. But on the whole, if they're well looked after and cared for they *do* respond and they *do* want a relationship with the person who is looking after them.'

I could not bear to go on thinking about it and turned all my attention to getting ready for when the plane arrived. It was due any minute and I desperately wanted to get away and to Buenos Aires as soon as possible.

I think the thing that astonished us as much as the animals' reluctance to see us go was the way Paula behaved. She had always been friendly, but up till now had seemed totally uninvolved. The Indians have a peculiar attitude; they treat all foreigners as though they do not exist and mean nothing to them; at least, on the surface this is how it appears. Now every one of her girls turned up and we were clasped to their heaving bosoms but it was when we got to Paula that we were nearly drenched in a stream of scalding tears.

She said that she had never before met 'gringos'

whom she had liked as much and that she did hope that we would come back to Paraguay, and that, if we *did* come, that we would stay with her and allow her to look after us once more. She went on and on in this vein until we became even more depressed, so it was with great relief that we saw the aircraft making its landing approach. This turned out to be a rather startling procedure, for not only was the little grass airstrip completely water-logged by the early rains, but also, we had been warned by our lorry driver that the pilot was totally mad and could never make a perfect landing. With this cheering thought in mind we piled into the little plane with Paula and the girls helping. Sarah sat on Gerry's lap and all the rest of the animals, even Pooh, behaved themselves perfectly. They seemed to know that we were escaping. The doors were finally slammed and we waved everyone good-bye. The pilot, as we taxied down the strip, did mention that he thought we were slightly overweight and that this might be a problem, particularly with all the water that was on the field. How right he was, for only after two hair-raising attempts did we finally get airborne.

'Well', he said cheerfully, 'we only have to get down now.'

Our lorry driver had not exaggerated, alas, for the landing that we did eventually make at Asunción was, I think, the most hair-raising experience that we had ever endured. As the plane pitched and tossed and all the warning lights and buzzers came on, we were convinced that the whole thing was going to flip over. Due to a miracle on somebody's part (certainly not the pilot's) we in the end came rather grudgingly to a halt. The door was wrenched open and an official of the company urged us to leave the plane as soon as possible. We must not delay for one second, as the aircraft that was to take us to Buenos Aires was waiting especially for us at Asunción Airport. Clambering into the waiting truck, we sped madly across to the other side of the city. Sure enough, there was the plane, with its engines warming up. Our friend and the other airline people brushed aside any enquiries from the odd official and it seemed that the next thing we really knew was that we were looking down at the twinkling lights of Buenos Aires beneath us.

I do not think we had ever felt so relieved. True to their reputation, all our friends were waiting for us at the airport. With the help of Mr Gibbs from the British Embassy, we eventually persuaded the Argentine officials to break every rule and regulation that had ever been made in order to let us and our animals through without the necessary pieces of paper. It was stretching their generosity to the extreme and it was touching that they were as concerned as we were that our animals should be whisked to warmth and comfort as soon as possible. Here again Bebita Ferreyra had come to our rescue and we were soon installed in a little house in the suburbs of Buenos Aires.

Over the next few days, we and our friends worked ceaselessly to construct new cages for the sea voyage.

Gerry made a brief visit to another estancia to try to augment our tiny collection. Also we visited the local animal dealers in the hope that they might have some interesting stuff. In this way, we had a not too inconsiderable menagerie to take back with us on the Blue Star freighter.

With great sadness and reluctance we finally bade farewell to all our dear friends who lined the quayside to wave us off.

Weeks later, on arrival in England, it was an even deeper sadness to say goodbye to our delightful creatures. Most of the animals went to Paignton Zoo, where, at that time, two people we knew very well were in charge. The rest went to London Zoo. It was particularly satisfactory that Cai, who was eventually presented with a mate, bred successfully. This is what looking after animals is all about – it is all very well to go out and collect them and to bring them back successfully, but you do not really justify any of this until your animal has finally bred.

Chapter Five

Penguins Galore

In 1958 we were lucky enough to go back to the Argentine. This time we had decided to concentrate on the remoter areas and, in particular, on that fascinating southern part of the country known as Patagonia. Unfortunately our second experience of arriving in Buenos Aires was not quite as trouble free as our first had been. There had, of course, been a change of government and naturally all the officials had changed at the same time. Thus we were presented with a bizarre situation, whereby the customs willingly let us have our Land-Rover, cine camera, recording machine, film, tapes and indeed all the really expensive equipment without any fuss whatsoever. For some unknown reason, however, they insisted on holding on (for six whole weeks) to the trailer which was full of our collecting gear and our old clothes. Without this camping and animal-catching gear, we simply could not operate. So began a tedious and long-drawn-out episode: an encounter with the family 'Garcia'. They seemed to be in complete control of the whole waterfront of Buenos Aires, and particularly of the customs. With a great deal of help from the more attractive members of our group of Argentine friends, we at last persuaded the ultimate Señor

Garcia to allow us to have the rest of the equipment.

During this period Gerry had not been exactly happy and, although one can say in complete honesty that living with him is never dull, particularly when one is in a foreign country and engaged upon animal collecting, I was never and indeed still never am prepared for the more eccentric exploits that he is liable to indulge in. I ask you, who else, when living in a small hotel in the middle of a large city like Buenos Aires, would encumber himself with a baby South American Tapir? He argued that it presented no problem, and that he was sure the hotel manager would share his fondness for wildlife and allow us to keep the tapir on the hotel roof. It was summer, there could be no difficulty. All we had to do was to erect some shade and the rest would be easy. Somehow, the manager could not really see it this way; he was courteous and polite but, as he reasonably pointed out, the roof of a hotel in the middle of Buenos Aires was hardly the place to keep a tapir, however small.

We had in fact found the tapir concerned in a dealer's front window in the middle of the city. Gerry could not resist him, which is not surprising because they are lovely, bulbous creatures, who have all the nicer characteristics of a dog and, when little, are covered in the most gorgeous white stripes and spots. 'Claudius' was just about to lose all these stripes and spots and so looked particularly endearing. We bundled him into the back of the Land-Rover and although immediately rebuffed by the hotel management, we were not to be defeated.

'Surely,' said Gerry, addressing all our friends, 'there must be some sanctuary where this poor orphaned creature could find a haven?'

The magic worked and one of our friends finally persuaded her mother to allow us to keep the tapir in their back garden. Buenos Aires is very like Paris, in as much as most people live in apartments, and so to have a garden was indeed a great privilege. Most people who had them took great pride in making them attractive, and this lady was no exception. She had a beautiful lawn and a passion for begonias, so I was very surprised that she finally agreed to let us keep a tapir there. Before she could change her mind, Gerry rushed round and Claudius was duly tethered in the middle of the garden. It was summer, so there was no reason to worry about the weather, and feeding him was very simple. Feeling that all was well, we patted Claudius fondly on the head and left.

Next morning, we got a heartfelt telephone call demanding that we go round to the house immediately.

'He's not ill, is he?' asked Gerry worriedly.

'Oh no, he's not ill, but I still think you ought to come,' said the daughter of the house.

On our arrival, we found, to our consternation, that Claudius had somehow or another broken free and had eaten half the precious begonias. Mama had retired with a headache and refused to have anything more to do with either the tapir or us or, indeed, her daughter. Claudius, in the meantime, had been persuaded to go to inspect the coal cellar where they promptly locked him in. We found him covered in coal dust, delicately munching a leaf. We scolded him thoroughly, telling him how naughty he had been and how unappreciative of all the great kindnesses that were being showered upon him. He appeared unable to appreciate our point of view. There seemed to be no alternative but to put him on a stout chain. We might as well not have troubled. That evening Claudius surpassed himself; he finished up the rest of the begonias. Naturally, we were in some doubt what to do next.

'How about a larger, stronger chain?' I volunteered.

'Also you'd better buy some begonias to pacify poor Mama,' said our worried friend.

We adopted both these tactics and left, fondly imagining that all would now be well. We had underestimated Claudius's ingenuity.

Next morning came the inevitable phone call.

'I'm afraid, Gerry,' said our friend, 'my mother insists that you remove Claudius.'

'Why, has he got up to even more mischief?' he asked anxiously.

It was obvious that our friend was trying desperately not to laugh at the other end of the telephone, and as she struggled to remain fairly serious, she went on to explain that her mother had given a rather important dinner party the night before. Just as they had all sat down to eat there was a dreadful noise in the garden. Somehow Claudius had managed to get free. Before they could do anything about it, he had burst in through the French windows, dragging the chain and staple and half the shrubbery behind him.

'Good God!' said Gerry.

Our friend could not contain herself any longer; she burst out laughing.

'You know, Gerry, I shouldn't say this, but it was *so* funny. All the guests were leaping about, obviously terrified, while Claudius ran round and round the table, clanking his chain. Then he got frightened by all their noise and did a large pile in the middle of the floor.'

Gerry groaned aloud. 'When I think what Claudius can really do in the way of decorating a floor,' he said, 'I can imagine what the mess must have been like.'

'My mother's reputation has been somewhat tarnished so she is decidedly angry. She also feels that Claudius is obviously unhappy in the garden, and she doesn't really find him very "*simpatico*".'

'Where is your mother now?' Gerry asked.

'Upstairs, and she's not feeling very friendly.'

'OK. Leave it to me, I'll think of something.'

Again a friend of a friend of a friend came to our rescue and we found suitable quarters for Claudius and someone who was prepared to take him on, bad habits and all. Perversely, he behaved so well whilst staying with this other person that she refused to believe that he deserved his ghastly reputation.

'He really is a dear, and I think he must have felt that the garden was perhaps too *formal* for him,' she said. 'Anyway, please don't hesitate to ask me to tapir-sit again.'

In the meantime the last piece of our clothing had been extricated from the hands of the customs and so, before anyone could change their minds and delay us further, we left the capital. Starting the new year in the right way, we departed on the morning of the 1st January. It was a subdued party that left the capital on that early morning, heads throbbing, tongues parched, and generally feeling feeble. The city was surprisingly quiet, even for that hour in the morning. Obviously, everyone was feeling like we did but, sensibly, had decided to stay in bed a little later.

We sped down the road on the first part of our journey. City-lovers always thought we were mad and those Argentines who lived in their great capital city simply could not understand visitors going off to look at the rest of the country, live rough and meet 'all these strange people'. Who knows, they might have guns and be unpleasant or even rude! They predicted all sorts of dire disasters. I cannot understand why; anyway, this sort of gloomy attitude has never deterred us in the least.

Once we had left the green pampas behind us the terrain became very different, almost alien. Patagonia, indeed all the southern half of the Argentine, has a special magic. It is often very cold, inhospitable and the wind blows straight up from the Antarctic, but it is a mysterious place, full of marvellous colours, strange people and even stranger animals. After five days of travelling, we eventually reached our destination, Puerto Deseado or 'the Port of Desire'. How anyone could possibly desire this particular habitation remained a mystery to everyone. It was bleak, miserable, cold and decidedly anti-foreign. The local people regarded anyone who was not an Argentine with the utmost suspicion, presumably because as wicked foreigners they might steal all their oil and not (as was indeed the case) help them get it out of the ground, so increasing the natural wealth of the country. The oil boom also made it virtually impossible to find anywhere to stay and we all had to spend the first night sleeping in our Land-Rover, not a comfortable experience.

Our contact was a Señor Huiche, on whose land a penguin colony nested. He turned out to be a charmer, half-Indian, who had, single-handed, built himself this unusual wooden dwelling by the sea, miles away from the township of Puerto Deseado. Bravely he agreed to look after our party. In the ensuing weeks he put up with the bother of having a horde of people around him who wanted to film, who got in his way, whom he had to feed, whom he had to guide. Never once did he complain, even when the smokers in the party ran out of cigarettes and used all his black tobacco to supply their needs. Nothing was too much trouble for this man; he did everything with a smile and with a charm and grace which we have seldom found in so-called educated people.

He showed us his marvellous collection of Indian relics, the flint arrow-heads and the various other pieces that he had found on his land. It had been an old Indian midden, or eating place, and so we found all manner of relics in the enormous dunes that bordered the property. It was at the foot of these dunes that the penguins lived and bred.

The colony stretched from the bottom of the rise, as far as the eye could see. It seemed that every square inch was inhabited by black and white shapes, and everywhere there was great activity. Apart from its astonishing size, the thing that was most apparent about this colovy, and that impinged upon one almost immediately, was the smell. I must say that for me bird smell is almost the nastiest of those few intangible and unpleasant disadvantages associated with our job. The smell that was coming from these penguins was extraordinary; a sickly, sweetish odour, with over-tones of fish, or rather, cod liver oil. I found it quite revolting.

The birds themselves, I soon realized, were without doubt the most stupid members of the bird family ever to come to my acquaintance, making the Guira Cuckoos look like embryo Einsteins. First of all, their burrows were often mere scrapes in the earth and placed far too close together. They had also decided to site their main breeding ground miles away from the actual sea – a flat area between the rise that we were standing on, and the extremely high sand dunes.

Doubtless the dunes protected them somewhat from the strong wind that was ever present but, in turn, they made the collection of food a Herculean task. The birds had to waddle on their tiny little legs all the way up the side of the steep slope, struggling through the soft flowing sand, often in the boiling sun. Once at the top they could toboggan down the other side, but another long walk then faced them before they reached the sea itself, which in turn was turbulent the whole time and hazardous in the extreme.

Not altogether surprisingly, we found that the mortality rate among the young of this colony was fantastically high. Everywhere were dehydrated corpses of baby birds, where sand, heat and hunger had assisted the usual marauders, like the gulls, who were always there hoping for easy pickings. I feared for the ultimate survival of this colony, but survive they certainly did and do. They bred in enormous numbers – we reckoned that in this area alone there were a million birds. Huiche, who had been studying the colony over the years, said that they seemed to have better results one year than another. He assumed that this was to do with the natural balance of nature and the food supply, although the coming of the oil wells, the oil tankers and the general development of the area, was bound to result in further casualties and, eventually, to the decline of the whole penguin colony in the area. He was equally concerned about the fate of the Elephant Seal and the Fur Seal, although, thanks to government embargoes, Fur Seal killing had been strenuously reduced practically to an uneconomic level and so would soon cease.

This was certainly something, yet it would do no good in the end if you could not also afford the animals protection from oil spills and, later, from the tourists. I am all for tourism as a means of preserving a species; it is sometimes economically vital and, if properly controlled, need do little harm. But when it reaches the proportions it apparently has in the case of the Elephant and Fur Seal colonies further north at Peninzula Valdez, it defeats its own object. There is now a critical problem caused both by the debris which the organized tours leave behind and their behaviour towards the colonies themselves – rock throwing and prodding with sticks. Equally disturbing stories are told about the Galapagos; visiting boats will dump their rubbish over the side and so the shoreline becomes strewn with that delight of civilization, the plastic bottle, as well as other debris.

On this particular trip, we concentrated on filming and not on catching animals. It was fascinating to have the time really to study these creatures and not to be concerned with the day-to-day care of a collection. Being involved with these colonies was an entirely new experience for us both, and a humbling one. Here they were living peacefully, at least providing territory was respected and mates were not enticed away. It was like living on a council estate; if you respected your neighbour's boundaries all went well, but woe betide you if you did not.

The Elephant Seals seemed to be rather lonely and more remote creatures than the Fur Seals, who were gay and abandoned and full of life. In the case of the latter, things were going on the whole time, in fact it was all we could do to stop Gerry using up every bit of film we had brought along. Reluctantly, we managed to tear ourselves away because it was time to return to the North. Now we planned to visit the western side of the Argentine, into the foothills of the Andes, Mendosa, then north again to places like Tucaman and JuJui, in the hope of getting a cross section of the fauna that lives in the whole country. So it was back to Buenos Aires in the steamy heat of February.

We decided to stop and have a snack in a remote village by the Rio Negro. It was an unkempt cafe but one of the younger members of the family rushed out to see what we wanted; perhaps some coffee or tea and a sandwich? He bowed timidly and darted back into the darkened back of the bar. While we waited we heard a funny gurgling noise from behind the door. Noise of any kind usually meant to us an animal, and we were not disappointed this time. There, standing very erect (or trying to) and bowing and clicking his beak, was a half-grown Burrowing Owl. These enchanting creatures live in burrows in the grasslands throughout the Argentine. They are among the most charming members of the bird family, and seem to have little fear of human beings. On further examination we noticed this particular bird had an injured foot. When the boy returned, clutching a pot of coffee and a plateful of sandwiches, we questioned him closely. It turned out that the owl belonged to the boy himself and was called Perico. The boy's father had been digging the adjoining land and had come across a whole family of Burrowing Owls. Strangely, he resisted the usual desire to destroy them. As a result of the digging, Perico had unfortunately been injured. The boy decided to keep him, for he was unable to fend for himself and risked ending up as a supper for one of the many hawks that inhabit the pampas.

Perico stood watching us, as stiff as any guardsman, then bowed up and down, very rapidly, to revert once more to his frozen guardsman-like stance. It was so funny that I am afraid we all rudely burst out laughing. Perico gave us a withering glare, shook himself grandly, nearly toppling over in the process, and glared at us with his lovely golden eyes. I remember that Ian Gibson had told us all about the Burrowing Owl, its habits and how useful it was because it lived basically off insects, beetles and other vermin, including the odd small rodent. I decided immediately that I must have this little bird. Gerry argued, quite rightly, that it was the boy's personal pet and that probably the last thing he would want to do was give it away. Somehow or other, however, the little boy seemed to realize that Perico and I had formed an understanding. When I offered a hand to the owl he immediately hopped on to it and allowed me to stroke him and tickle his head. His eyes slowly closed and he went off into a trance-like stupor. He was pretty to look at, being a mixture of gingery-brown feathering, flecked with white and approximately six inches in height – Gerry said that he would not grow much more.

Then began a determined campaign by my dear spouse to try to persuade me that transporting an owl all the way to Buenos Aires and keeping it in a hotel was ludicrous in the extreme. I carefully reminded him of all the trials and tribulations we had undergone with Claudius, and insisted that, by comparison, Perico would be no trouble at all.

'It's no use going on. If I can persuade this child to let me have the owl, I'm determined to take him back.'

Seeing that he was making no headway Gerry gave in and we began our negotiations.

I think the little boy realized how much I wanted his pet and I like to think that we did not bring too much pressure on him to sell. At last a bargain was struck. I gathered Perico in my hands and walked out to the Land-Rover.

On the two-day trip to Buenos Aires, Perico perched on the back of my seat. Whenever possible we got him minced meat, which I mixed with cotton wool as roughage. If meat was not available, we gave him bits of hard-boiled egg and biscuits, all mixed up together and rolled into little balls to be inserted into Perico's mouth. He accepted everything with complete aplomb, as though travelling around in a Land-Rover had been the one thing that he had always wanted to do.

Arriving back in the hotel, it was simplicity itself to install him in our room. I think by this time the manager had become inured to us and overlooked our eccentric behaviour. Our friends in the capital were intrigued by Perico and he held court twice a day. Every morning they came round to see how they could help us make arrangements to move on to the North; Perico seemed to realize that they were interested in him and his well-being and graciously accepted their gifts of cockroaches or any other insect life that they could find. One friend used to bring tiny pieces of minced beef especially for him and another brought us a lot of chicken feathers. It is vital for owls to have this roughage in order to keep their whole systems oiled, as it were. It is necessary for owls to regurgitate things like little bones or pieces of insect casing wrapped up in the feathers or fur. This casting, as it is called, is an integral part of the digestive system of the owl family and they are not healthy unless they do it regularly.

All this attention and love, strangely enough, did not spoil Perico or go to his head; he accepted it as normal and proper. Our friends had not quite realized the charm of owls and before long we had a constant stream of visitors. At first I worried lest this might be a bad thing for the little bird, but, on the contrary, he thrived on it. Even the maids who came in to clean the rooms were fascinated by him. He would sit on the end of my bed while everybody was cleaning and talking and then, if I put him down on the floor, would potter about, click his beak, bob up and down and generally have a good time.

Our plans to go north went ahead rapidly, then suddenly I began to feel ill. Just before we had gone to Patagonia we had unluckily been involved in a car crash. A friend had been driving us and, being rather volatile, had not concentrated on the road and did not notice the lights turning red. All I remember was shouting 'Lights!' and then being catapulted into the windscreen, hitting something solid. I was not immediately aware of being hurt in any way until, suddenly, my vision clouded. I kept asking, 'Have we damaged the Land-Rover, have we damaged the Land-Rover?' which was not perhaps the most important issue at that moment. Yet I was not wholly absurd, for without this vehicle we were powerless to go anywhere, cars being scarce in the Argentine. It seemed almost as if our visits to South America were doomed: on the first trip the revolution had caused havoc; this time we had been delayed by the customs; the last thing we needed was a crash.

Through a red mist, I heard voices; apparently we had hit an army general and he was deeply distressed at the sight of me deluged in blood. I could hear him asking if we needed any help. The last thing I wanted was a lot of fuss, but this, of course, is just what I got. The wound in my forehead was cleaned at the nearby clinic and then stitched. I was told to go home and take it easy for the next 24 hours and to come back in a week's time for the stitches to be taken out.

Next day I gracefully collapsed in the middle of a restaurant; the one and only time I have ever done this. Another medical man diagnosed severe concussion, nothing more. The stitches were in due course removed and we had left for the south. The Patagonian roads had not helped and by the time we got back to Buenos Aires in February, I really did feel ghastly and unable to continue the trip. Gerry had lots of people to help him and I knew that nothing could go wrong, so I caught the next boat back to England with Perico as my companion.

The Royal Mail ship had a very understanding captain and he allowed me to keep the owl in my bathroom. At night I would leave the door open so that Perico could have the run of the cabin as well, which he thoroughly enjoyed. The cabin steward was immediately captivated and, along with my morning cup of tea, produced a saucer of finely chopped best Argentine beef and some feathers – with the chef's compliments. At first light Perico, who slept all night, would suddenly appear at my bedside, chirruping madly and clicking his beak, demanding to be made much of. The steward's appearance caused great excitement – for it meant feeding time. In this way, Perico and I spent a very happy three weeks.

Back in Bournemouth, the Durrell family welcomed us both enthusiastically and permitted Perico the run of the entire house. Throughout his long life Perico continually attracted admirers and was deeply mourned when he died many years later. But in spite of all his other fans, he steadfastly remained mine to the end.

Chapter Six

Small Beef

The African continent has never exercised for me the same fascination as South America and later Australasia, but nevertheless I was intrigued by the idea of revisiting Gerry's old stamping-ground, the then British Cameroons. As Gerry had allowed me to choose the venue for our first trip together, it was only right that he should be allowed the same privilege for our second trip which took place in 1956. Gerry had been to this area twice before and loved both it and its people.

The Cameroons were full of the most fascinating creatures; things like hairy frogs, flying mice and Angwantibos, as well as the usual animals such as monkeys and chimpanzees, plus a wide variety of snakes and lovely birds like plantain-eaters, hornbills and flamingos. They all sounded very bizarre yet as much as any of them I looked forward to meeting the Fon or chief of Bafut, whom Gerry had immortalized in his third book, *The Bafut Beagles*.

When I first heard about the Fon I had had a sneaking suspicion that Gerry was using a bit of poetic licence to describe his character and the details of their encounter. I was soon to learn that it was far from an exaggeration – in fact, if Gerry had written about the

Fon as he really was, I do not think anyone would have believed a single word.

Again, I was given the slightly unenviable task of preparing for our trip to West Africa. This time we were to go further north into gorilla country in the hope of filming and catching gorilla. We had experimented with a dart gun and had had fruitful discussions about this project with various friends in the drug and ballistic fields. Alas, we were not able to perfect an idea which has since been developed and proved a boon to wildlife people throughout the world. At the Trust we have used the drug gun to great effect both in the transport and the treatment of animals, thus reducing stress considerably.

As this was going to be an important expedition, we solicited the help of various British manufacturers. In a standard letter we offered, in return for their help, to provide photographs of their various products in use in the field (I do feel that our secretary at the time rather overdid things when she wrote to ask Jeyes for lavatory paper). The response was overwhelming and when we finally sailed for West Africa, we looked rather like the old African traders, only this time, instead of beads, salt and Toby jugs, we were taking Dexian for cage building, Bovril, Horlicks, Complan, and Mr Tetley's teabags, as well as Tilley lamps and safari beds. There was hardly a single item that you could think of that was not represented in our baggage, for we had to be completely self-supporting.

Our arrival at Victoria in the Cameroons early in January 1957 was something of a shock as far as I was concerned. Although I had realized that, as the area was tropical, it would be hot and probably moist, I was quite unprepared for the steamy blanket which enfolded the ship as she dropped anchor. I had never been in a place – not even Buenos Aires, which was pretty unbearable in February – where I have been so acutely uncomfortable. No movement was necessary to drench you in perspiration and it was impossible to keep cool. Gerry assured me that I would get used to it, but I never did, and I think it was only my deep interest in the animals that really enabled me to see that six months through.

I had been warned about the adventures of travelling up-country in what are called 'Mammy Waggons'. These Bedford or Ford trucks fitted with wooden seats in the rear were the life-blood of the Cameroons at that time, and had wonderful names like 'Godspeed'. The bargaining for lorry hire was unbelievable, but a necessary part of life. Gerry had warned me about all this but I could not get used to the prolonged and noisy haggling. Eventually an agreement was reached and we were ready to set off.

The road as far as Kumba was paved, so this part of the journey was not too bad, but after the town it became laterite. Soon we were covered in thick red dust. The first stage in our journey up-country was Mamfe but Gerry was anxious to have a break in Bakebe village in order to pick up a couple of his old animal boys and pay his respects to the local chief. The chief greeted Gerry warmly and insisted that we have a glass of beer with him, while he sent the boys off to find a hunter who had already got an animal. Gerry was intrigued by this and could not wait to get his hands on it. When it eventually arrived it proved to be something that made him wild with delight, a baby Black-footed Mongoose, quite a rarity. Christened 'Tikki', she was covered from nose to tail in a lovely creamy white fur, but the four little legs were black, as were her nose and eyes.

The man refused to be parted from his sack and so it became obvious that the only way we could transport Tikki was by carrying her in the cab. Having paid the man the agreed price, thanked the chief warmly, and made contact again with all the old hunters, we reluctantly got back into the truck. Tikki was proving quite a handful, as she did not really appreciate the smell of diesel and engine noise. Gerry decided to pop her into his shirt. We spent the rest of the journey with Gerry juggling madly; shouts of 'Ow!' or 'Keep still you little devil!' alternating with crooning and affectionate patting. All in all we were very exhilarated by our first acquisition.

The thing that has always struck me forcibly is how two animals of the same species, reared identically, can differ so much in character and in their attitude to human beings. Tikki, our first Black-footed Mongoose, had never deviated in her warmth and friendliness towards us, and loved nothing better than to be stroked, played with and taken for walks on the end of a leash. So imagine how delighted we were when the Forestry Officer appeared one day with a second baby Black-footed Mongoose. She was smaller than Tikki, being about two feet in length and standing about eight inches in height, and was slightly creamier in colour. We decided to call her 'Tavi'.

Unlike Tikki, the last thing that this newcomer wanted was to have anything to do with us. The Forestry Officer had found her in a nest which had obviously been abandoned by the mother and, being worried about the youngster, thought that the least he could do was to bring her in. She had apparently accepted the help with resignation if no real enthusiasm, but she soon gave us to understand, very firmly, that we were merely providers of security and food. If we expected anything further than this, it was our bad luck. The extraordinary thing was that they both stuck to their respective outlooks throughout their very long lives: Tikki, exuberant, ebullient and friendly; Tavi, reserved, cold and remote.

Tired, exhausted and dirty, we arrived at the UAC compound. In West Africa, the United Africa Company ran the trading system throughout the west coast and we had been invited to stay at the Mamfe manager's house. Since Gerry's day, a new bungalow had been built, rather a swish affair, overlooking the river. Drawing up by the lighted veranda, we could see three men sitting round a table deeply engrossed in their card game.

'Wait here,' said Gerry, 'and I'll go in and find out what's what.'

I heard Gerry say, 'Good evening, my name is Durrell.'

One of the men immediately leapt to his feet, rushed over, shook him by the hand and said,

'I say, old boy, do you play Canasta?'

This was equal to the Livingstone–Stanley meeting. The man who had made this memorable remark was John Henderson, the UAC manager, who invited us to take possession of his house. He must have bitterly regretted his generosity over the next few months for he disliked animals and yet our main preoccupation was to infest the surroundings of his house with as many species as we could lay our hands on.

Interviewing the Africans was apt to be amusing because, although they were quite knowledgeable when pressed, they were always vague. When you asked, 'What you go get for dis bag?' immediately it would be, 'Nah beef, sah.' 'Beef' is the blanket word in West Africa, meaning anything from a beetle to a gorilla, and you had to probe deeply to find out what it was with which you were liable to be faced when you opened a sack or a box. It was often a hair-raising experience. When faced with a box, we did not immediately rush to open it or stick our hands in it because we were quite liable to be bitten by a deadly snake or an irate member of the cat family.

The word had spread like wildfire that 'Massa Dul-lel' was back and that we wanted 'plenty beef'.

Soon the hunters were forming queues at our door. One of the first arrivals turned out to be one of those special characters whom you always long for on an expedition of this sort, especially if you are thinking in filmic terms.

Opening our first sack and being assured, after pressure, that it was a monkey, Gerry was delighted to find gazing at him from the depths a small grey face, with huge ears and eyes. Eagerly, Gerry inserted his hand and retrieved a delightful creature which had large, very human hands, complete with small flat nails except for the forefinger, which had a curved claw.

'This,' said Durrell, 'is something I've been trying to get on every trip to the Cameroons.'

'Well, what is it?' I asked, not being clairvoyante.

'It's known as a Needle-clawed Lemur, or Bush-baby. They are very, very rare and it would probably be a first time importation if we could land it safely in Britain.'

The hunter assured us that they all knew the 'beef' well and they had seen it lots of times.

'Yes,' said Gerry, 'Now you go tell all the people of your village that I go pay one pound for dis beef, you hear?'

'Yes sah, I go tell 'em,' he said.

On closer examination, we found it even more charming than it at first appeared, for its enormous ears could be folded back alongside its head. For some unknown reason the name 'Bugs' immediately came

1. Eggbert the Screamer. His body was roughly the size of a coconut and at the end of a long neck was a high, domed intellectual forehead.

2. Cai the Douracoulis. Enormous owl-like eyes, a beautiful pale amber colour, were edged with white fur tipped in black

3. One of the armadillo twins

4. Pooh the crab-eating Raccoon. A mask of black fur across the eyes made him look like a comic burglar

5. A Guira Cuckoo — one of the most ridiculous birds I have ever met

6. The Fon of Bafut. Magnificent to look at. Well over six feet in height but very slender

7. Npongo, the baby gorilla, being introduced to our boxer dog, Keeper

8. Whiskers the Emperor Tamerin

9. Miffy the spot-nosed monkey

10. Timothy the Ground Squirrel.
My most outstanding pet.

into mind and so he was named. He quickly became a superior member of our collection. He got ridiculously tame and loved nothing better than to be picked up, cuddled, tickled and made a fuss of generally. Feeding was really no problem; he readily took to fruits and, of course, any insects that we were lucky enough to find. One night we had an invasion of flying ants. Everything and everyone were covered in these all-pervasive creatures. Through the swarming insects we could see Bugs's cage was stuffed with them, and so was he. His mouth was full, both hands were full, and his eyes (which had grown to about three times their normal size) were riveted on the hosts of flying insects. Every other insect-eater in the collection was having a marvellous time as well; it was rather like children being inundated with lollipops. They just had not got enough hands or mouths to hold all the treats that they were offered.

After we had cleaned out his cage and placed new leaves and sawdust in the bottom, one of Bugs's favourite games was to be picked off his branch, very gently of course, placed on his back, and tickled on his tummy. He would roll about gurgling with pleasure until he was thoroughly exhausted. If I left my hand in the box he would start to play with it to indicate that he wanted to be tickled again.

I have always had a particular interest in rodents and, even more, in the squirrel family. Gerry had assured me that Africa was teeming with squirrels of all varieties, shapes and colours. So far, not one of the 'beef' brought into the camp had proved to be a squirrel and I was getting to the state where I did not believe him any more.

As we were cleaning out one morning a large man appeared on the veranda carrying a raffia bag. The usual session began.

'Nah whatee der for inside,' Gerry began.

'Nah Squillil, sah,' the man replied.

'What is a Squillil?' I asked, puzzled.

'I haven't the faintest idea,' replied Gerry. 'Nah whatee dis Squillil?'

'Nah small beef, sah.'

'E bad beef?'

'No sah, dis Squillil nah pickin'.'

This seemed to satisfy Gerry for he bent down, untied the top of the bag, then gave me a smug, satisfied look before putting his hand inside. When he pulled it out, curled up in his palm, in a nest of grass, lay a tiny baby squirrel. It could not have been more than about three inches long and was still blind and covered in the very short, plushy fur that baby squirrels have. I was captivated.

'Well,' said Gerry warningly, 'they're not easy things to hand-rear, and this little thing can't be very old, so don't get too attached to it because, ten to one, it will die. But if you really want to have a go, I'll bargain.'

'He seems to be strong and I think it's worth trying, so let's have it. I promise I won't ask you for any help or advice about how to look after it, and I won't moan if, in the end, it does die.'

After a long discussion, it was agreed that the hunter would take half the money now and come back in a week for the rest. This seemed a perfectly good bargain to him because, looked at purely from a food point of view, the baby squirrel would not even have been worth cooking. Apparently he had killed the mother for food and later found the nest with just this one baby in it.

On closer examination, I could see that its tiny head was bright orange, with a neat black rim behind each ear. The body was a brindle green on the back and pale yellow on the tummy and the tiny tail was almost dark green above and flame orange below. She was promptly christened 'Squillil Small' – this later became abbreviated to 'Small', otherwise one had to engage in endless explanations as to what a 'squillil' was.

I decided that the best thing to do was to keep it warm and feed it as often as possible. To begin with I stuck it down my bra; after all, there it was warm and handy. I had had experience in South America with a special Humming Bird mixture and I was convinced that this would also do for hand-rearing babies. It was very simple, equal parts of Horlicks, Complan, Nestlé's milk, a touch of Bovril and a quarter of a teaspoonful of glucose, mixed together into a milky consistency plus a multi-vitamin. This I fed Small with the aid of an eye-dropper, for the little animal's mouth was so small that none of the teats we had brought with us would do. Sometimes one can substitute heavily soaked cotton wool, but the danger there is that odd strands might be sucked in and cause asphyxiation.

The little squirrel immediately adopted me as its mother and was never really any trouble, except when it was hungry. She would cling to my hand as I rested the end of the dropper on the ball of my thumb, thus giving herself the feeling that she was close to her mother. She was a messy feeder, very greedy, and would often half choke herself or get the food all over her fur. I cured this by wrapping her in a paper tissue, which at least absorbed some of her droppings. There is one especial danger I have found when hand-rearing these babies. For some unknown reason they seem very prone to renal failure. Often, just when you think you are over the hump with the squirrel and it is doing well, it will suddenly collapse, or rather its kidneys will, and it will be dead in a short space of time. This is heart-breaking, and I deliberately checked myself from getting too optimistic about Small, just in case.

We had several other types of squirrel brought into us, of varying ages and sizes, and they all did equally well, but none of them had the warm and lovable characteristics of Small. She was intelligent and utterly delightful. When she grew a little and her eyes opened, she came to recognize me. By this time it was impossible to keep her in my bra any more – apart from her increasing size her claws were growing and it could be decidedly uncomfortable. Also, I never knew when she was going to pop out. It could happen that I would be cleaning a cage containing quite a ferocious animal and she might leap out almost into its jaws. Gerry suggested that, between feeds, she should be put into a box of some kind. John Henderson donated a biscuit tin, which was converted into a squirrel house. Even though it was hot, I was worried that she might catch a chill, so a hot-water bottle was first placed in the box; this, in its turn, was covered by a strip of grey cotton blanket – also provided through the kindness of John Henderson; on to this, in turn, was placed a bedding of cotton wool and into the centre of all this Small was inserted. At night the box was covered with mosquito netting (to prevent her from leaping all over the room and waking everybody up), and put either on my bed or on my bedside table; it was not safe to leave animals on the floor in case of an invasion by driver ants, those horrifying creatures that devour everything in their path.

So it was that Small became an integral part of our existence. Even John Henderson was captivated by her and never failed to make daily enquiries as to her progress. On the whole, she was extremely well behaved, except for times when she thought I was a bit tardy with her food. I decided to go on bottle-feeding her and, although I did occasionally offer her the odd bit of mashed banana and other soft fruits, the basis of her diet remained the Humming Bird mixture.

We rose early in the morning, because it was relatively cooler at dawn than later on in the day and we wanted to do our cleaning out of the animals before breakfast. As Small got older, I decided that she could wait a little longer for her first feed. I soon learnt that she had no intention of being neglected in this manner. We were busily cleaning out, all of us engrossed in what we were doing, when suddenly I heard a very peremptory 'chirrup, chirrup'. I was startled, because I could not imagine where this noise was coming from. Again, 'chirrup, chirrup'; it got nearer and nearer. Eventually it turned out to be Small. Having clambered out of her biscuit box and found that I had gone, she had come to find me outside on the veranda. This was no mean feat for a little squirrel, because, in order to get to us from our bedroom, she had had to find the bedroom door, come along a corridor, go through the living-room and out on to the veranda. Gerry was amused by this but insisted that it was really about time that she had a proper box where she could play and generally occupy herself. Also, he felt that the time had come for her to have a more solid diet and a little more protein than the mixture was giving her.

With loving care, we constructed a beautiful tall cage, with a sleeping box at the top, a lovely branch inside and lots of playing area. Small adored this box and eventually got to the point where she would only come out as a special favour to me. Otherwise, her day was spent inspecting every inch of the cage, especially after I had cleaned it out and put in fresh leaves and sawdust. Of course food pots were always vigorously pounced upon and inspected, but it was her nest box that was really her own kingdom.

To begin with, we put in a layer of sawdust to absorb the urine and any fruit juice that she might bring in. On top of this, we put dried banana leaves, crumpled up. Then, in order to give her some bedding and something to play with, I introduced a couple of paper handkerchiefs. This caused a riot. She pounced on them, and ran up and down the branch with them stuffed into her mouth. Not being pleased with the texture, she patted them, pulled them, shredded them, put them into her mouth, pulled them out again and ran around the cage until, finally satisfied that all the newness had been beaten out of them, she rushed up into the bedroom. With a lot of scratching and scraping the tissues were then very carefully torn into tiny pieces and made into a little nest. After all this fevered activity, she appeared in the entrance, looking exhausted but with an expression on her face that left me in no doubt that something was still missing. I was forced to the conclusion that she needed more bedding, so I offered her another paper handkerchief. With this she promptly covered up the hole leading to her nest. In fact, all she wanted was a curtain over her front door so that she could have total privacy. A firm understanding was reached; I never intruded into her box until the little curtain had been pulled aside.

The nest box I checked daily to see that it was dry and did not need any fresh leaves or bits of paper, but the once-a-week thorough clean-out (which I felt was necessary if any hygiene was to be maintained), was always a traumatic experience. Small was obviously torn between her inclination to give in to me, because she knew that I meant her no harm, and her grave reluctance to have her little domain invaded and all her lovely smelly bits removed.

Gerry always teased me about my relationship with Small, but he was also captivated by her and on the boat journey back to Liverpool allowed her to spend a lot of time in the cabin, pottering about and investigating the bed. Never once did she have any inclination to wander further afield. Although totally 'my' squirrel, she would tolerate Gerry, and the attention of others, especially when there was the offer of a succulent grasshopper or cricket.

My depression on being forced to leave her with friends when we left for the Argentine in 1958 was indescribable and the news of her death, from virus pneumonia, was horrible. I swore never again to become too involved with a particular animal, it was too painful.

Chapter Seven

Fon and Frolics

I feel I cannot write about our West African visit without mentioning my encounter with the Fon of Bafut. When we felt we had exhausted the possibilities of the animals around Mamfe, Gerry decided to accept the Fon's pressing invitation to go up to the mountains and visit him in Bafut. So it was that we and our animals were transported by truck, up the road to Bafut and eventually settled in the Fon's famous rest house within his compound in the main village.

The rest house was a lovely old building, consisting of two storeys, with a wide veranda bisecting it. In the lower, mud-floored rooms, we stored all our equipment, while we actually lived on the first floor.

The Fon agreed that we could keep animals on the veranda, thus having them under our eyes, as it were, for 24 hours a day. This had the great advantage that it was very unlikely that any Driver Ant column would wend their way up to this level. The Fon was delighted to have Gerry back and greeted him enthusiastically, insisting that we go inside his dancing house.

'Welcome, welcome, we go for inside,' he said.

Gerry flourished a large bottle of whisky that he had brought over.

'I never go empty-handed to the Fon's', he said. 'He's

such a generous man. After all, we live here, we have all the protection that the Fon can offer and his people will do anything for us, so the least I can do is show my appreciation by taking him presents.'

The Fon was magnificent to look at, well over six feet in height but, although a big man, very slender, with long delicate-looking feet and extremely nice hands, well shaped and well looked after. These hands would not have disgraced any woman, and I think, secretly, he was rather vain about them. He was dressed in a long multi-coloured robe, worn over a white smock, and on his head was the knitted hat that is typical of this region of the Cameroons. Perched incongruously on the end of his nose were his 'granny glasses'. He was completely bald, but this seemed to add to his attraction. He had a keen sense of humour, a lovely uproarious laugh, and a ridiculous giggle.

That he was fond of Gerry was obvious from the start, as he threw his arms round him, patted him, and recalled all their good times together, especially the famous occasion when Gerry had taught the Fon's wives to do the 'Conga', which he promised we would do again before we left his kingdom. His reaction to me was startling. He had obviously been warned that Gerry now had a wife and he kept giving me rather shy but curious looks. I think it was a measure of how well we got on that, before we actually left Bafut, he once announced to me; 'You'd be foine wife for me. My wives they humbug me too much.' Having as many of these as he did, his statement was hardly surprising.

He was obviously a despot, in the true meaning of the word, but he nevertheless appeared to rule his people with gentle shrewdness, appreciating all their failings and yet wanting to improve their lot in a moderate and understanding way. However, it was rumoured that he was not above having any opposition quietly removed. I think it proves the shrewdness of the man that, when asked whether to advise union with Nigeria or with what was then the French Cameroons, he opted for the French Cameroons. As he said:

'Nigeria nah fire, French Cameroons, nah water' – This cryptic statement was made not very long before the outbreak of the Nigerian civil war.

It was with great sadness that we heard of the Fon's death, from an American lady who had recently visited Bafut. It touched us deeply that he boasted to her of the book that had been written which had made him famous all over the world, *The Bafut Beagles*, and that he stressed how deeply he valued Gerry's friendship, which he underlined by making him a deputy Fon. I believe this is a privilege that was granted to few – if any – other Europeans, and was particularly surprising, as the Fon never made any secret of the fact that he was not over-enthusiastic about Europeans in general.

Nothing was too much trouble. When we were filming he not only allowed us to use his own personal

Land-Rover but stood for hours in the blazing sun while we took photographs of him. When a *Time-Life* photographer joined us he extended his fullest co-operation. One always had to remind oneself that this man had the status of royalty in his own country. We will always treasure the carved figure that he presented to Gerry on his first visit to Bafut. It was intended to be a good luck symbol, and I think, on the whole, Gerry would agree that it seems to have worked its magic for him. It will always be a memento of a great friendship.

Soon we were inundated with creatures and the problem was to decide what to accept and what to turn away. All the time we reminded ourselves that these people hunted the animals for food and so we were saving the life of a creature if we decided to take it. It was not as if we encouraged them to go to look for the animals and then refused to take them off their hands.

A great variety of creatures inhabited that region and it was not long before we had, amongst other things, a baby Black and White Civet cat. These creatures, when adult, are extremely handsome; their bodies are about two and a half feet long and they have a tail of about eighteen inches. The fur is ashy-grey with enormous black spots and stripes and the tail itself is ringed black and white. Our new arrival was this in miniature and, of course, rather fluffy. He reminded me very much of Pooh, the South American Raccoon. He was quite obviously distressed at being man-handled and was crying loudly, so we immediately put him into a covered box; this way we hoped to restore his sense of security and to calm him down generally. Happily this worked. He always had tremendous spirit and, although he did not really mind being stroked, he objected strongly to being picked up.

We always checked thoroughly every animal we received, because, believe me, Mother Nature is not all that benevolent. You will often get creatures brought to you that are on the border of starvation or riddled with internal and external parasites, covered in ticks and, often, running sores; this apart from any wounds that the ham-handed hunters might have inflicted. So an animal had to be carefully inspected to make sure that it was in good condition. Should we find anything, treatment was begun immediately and might be prolonged.

The process of getting this baby civet to accept our various ministrations often ended up with us being covered in scratches and bites, but the reward was worth all the struggle and stress. Soon he became calmer and readily accepted any tit-bit we cared to give him. The boys often found Weaver Birds' eggs and these were an excellent source of additional protein for both the squirrels and the usual egg-eating animals, like civets. Yet it was bananas that held a particular fascination for Leeki as we called him. He regarded them as living things. Civets often kill by not only biting their prey but also falling on it with their shoulders, and to see Leeki killing a banana in this fashion was uproarious. As it appeared under the feeding slot of the cage, he would pounce upon it, drag it right in, sniff it gingerly, then fall sideways on to it, rather like a wrestler falling on an opponent. This would go on until he was satisfied that it was 'dead'. By this time the skin had burst so that both Leeki and the bottom of the cage were covered in squashed banana.

Back in Jersey, after a long search, we eventually found him a mate. These two went on to have an enormous number of babies and Leeki himself created a longevity record, so I think on reflection, one would agree that captivity has something to be said for it. If we had not taken him he certainly would have been eaten by the native hunter and so have deprived the world of 25 other civets.

Naturally, in this area, a lot of chimpanzees came our way. Some, unfortunately, were beyond any help that we could give them. On paper, the chimpanzee is a strictly protected animal in the Cameroons, but the Africans, who actually fear this rather hysterical ape, continued to hunt it for food. One method used widely was steel-wire trapping – a barbarous practice. I disapprove of traps of any kind, particularly because innocent victims like birds and the smaller mammals often hang in nooses for days, suffering the most painful deaths. The old-fashioned method of bow and arrow had at least the merit of more often than not killing the prey instantly.

A fully-grown chimp was brought to us, having been caught in a trap. Its wrists were cut through to the bone and gangrenous. We also noted an unusual condition – a weird kind of torpor. Fortunately we were only some sixteen miles away from the main administrative town, Bemenda, which boasted both a doctor and a vet who had shown great interest in the medical aspects of our animals and asked if they might be notified of anything that we thought interesting. Going into Bemenda next day for additional supplies, we naturally contacted them both and they promised to come out later to see the chimpanzee. The two men did everything they could to save the animal and when it eventually died their post-mortem examinations and tests revealed that the animal had, in fact, been suffering from sleeping sickness in an advanced state. Probably it would not have survived long even if we had managed to arrest the spread of the gangrene.

One of the local planters, a Dutchman, offered us his tame female chimp, the only condition being that we caught her first. She had never been shut up but lived in a large compound near his house. Undaunted by this challenge, we set off, with a cage, in the Fon's Land-Rover. 'Minnie', as she was called, was in many ways an engaging character, but she proved to be difficult to catch. It took poor old Durrell a whole day to persuade her gently to come into the crate, using such ruses as sitting in the crate himself (pretending to like it very much) holding a stem of bananas or standing on his head. Gradually he gained her confidence and eventually persuaded her that it might even be fun to go into the box with him. We had so designed the slides at each end that they would close when we pulled on ropes, and so, once she was inside, it was relatively easy to keep her there. She spent the trip back to the Fon's house with her arm stretched through the bars of the crate, plucking bananas from a large stem that we had hung above her.

Our animal boys adored her, mainly because of her ridiculous habits. Apart from being very friendly and wanting to be played with, one of her favourite tricks was to place her brightly coloured plastic food bowls on her head. She would sometimes have as many as six or seven balanced there at one time. Having achieved this feat she would then clap her hands and screech until she had an audience to admire her handiwork. This screeching was indeed her main drawback, especially as there was often no apparent reason for such a display. The only way to get peace was to employ somebody practically full time to keep her amused.

Two other chimpanzees that came our way were rather younger. One, Rupert, was a weak little thing. In spite of the efforts of ourselves, the doctor and the vet, nothing we did provided him with the incentive to live. No foods we could offer seemed to suit him and in the end he literally wasted away. Both vet and doctor were of the opinion that he had some sort of malfunction in his system which prevented him from taking food.

Later, just as we were about to leave Bafut, our last and, perhaps, most characterful chimpanzee arrived in our midst – Chumley. He had been sent up all the way, by UAC wagon, from down-country and he arrived squeaking and squalling, as only baby chimpanzees can. He had a bright, intelligent face and an obvious strength of will, which was going to pose great problems to us in the future. He and Gerry took to one another immediately, which pleased me because, to be honest, I do not really care for apes and monkeys and so have not this great affection for chimpanzees that seems to afflict most people. I know that they have funny ways and that they are close to the human, but they are also hysterical and, in my experience, unreliable; unlike most animals. Perhaps a little too human for my liking, in fact, often displaying the more tiresome of human characteristics in place of the more solid animal qualities.

It was a great relief to me not to be lumbered with Chumley full time, although I did my stint of feeding, cleaning and playing with him, particularly when we got to Bournemouth and the Durrell family house. He could not live outside with the other animals because he was susceptible to chest colds. Inevitably, he was adopted as another member of the family. Gerry's mother, sister and secretary all thoroughly spoiled him and gave him no discipline whatsoever, which proved disastrous. Everything he did that was mischievous was dismissed as being just child-like behaviour and he was not to be admonished because, as they said in their Spock-like way, he was only a baby. The fact that the two people he did respect were those who maintained some sort of discipline (Gerry and myself) underlines strongly that young apes need firmness. Further evidence of this is surely to be found in the fact that all our great apes chastise their children in a severe manner and administer blows which, if given to a human child, would immediately make the parent liable to prosecution under the various child protection acts.

To illustrate further: we have had a recent experience with orang-utan mothers who both reared their children successfully. One was a possessive and silly mother, the other sensible and unconcerned, in as much as her infant was encouraged, right from the beginning, to be independent and not to look upon his mother, or father, as being essential to his well-being. They played with him, fed him, comforted him when he was worried or when he hurt himself, but if he wished to go off on his own, that was fine by them. Eventually things got to the point where the little creature would be suspended high on the bars of the cage whilst the parents were below, calmly eating their food. None of the parties concerned were in any way distressed and the baby knew that if he was really in difficulties they would come to his aid. They, in turn, knew that he was quite capable of fending for himself.

In the next-door cage, quite the reverse was happening – instead of the mother being firm with her offspring she let it do what it liked, until eventually, when it was weaned, it was opening her mouth and stealing her food. She ended up with a baby that was spoilt beyond belief and a nasty-tempered creature at that.

We have since encouraged these two babies to associate with each other. The relationship has proved to be rather intriguing. The spoilt, dependent female clings to the slightly smaller but independent male. This is not a good thing from his point of view, but we hope that in time the other will get better. It is also interesting to see the characteristics of naughtiness appearing in the spoilt youngster and not in the independent one. This seems to me to have relevance in today's human society – for I have always maintained that, even though it may have a financially deprived background, given the right kind of discipline and a good relationship with a parent, no child will be a problem.

To return to Bafut; having had Bugs, the Bushbaby, I naturally looked forward to acquiring other members of this family. In the Bafut area are to be found the tiniest of all the Bushbabies, called Demidoff's. You can imagine my delight when I was presented with four Demidoff's babies. Even when fully grown, two adult Demidoff's barely fill a teacup. There is apparently great colour variation; ours tended to be olive grey with lighter underparts, and the fur was soft and thick and gorgeous to the touch. They have the usual enormous golden eyes, naked ears and charming pointed noses. By this time, we had quite a collection of squirrels and mice, all of which were newly born, and having, by this time, perfected my hand-rearing technique my success rate was extremely high. Carrying them around next to my body so as to keep them warm the whole time, plus hot water bottles, blankets and cotton wool, and also the liberal use of the Tilley infra-red paraffin heater that we had brought with us especially for this purpose, were definite factors in our satisfactory results. Being able to devote a lot of time to feeding at regular intervals is also vital when dealing with these tiny mammals.

By the time these Demidoff's arrived I had quite a family already, all clamouring to be fed. Even staggering the feeding times left little time for anything else, but at least all my babies were well cared for. I found it easier to have two babies in the hand at one time. Clasping them gently in my left hand so that their front paws stuck out over the top of my thumb, I could feed a full dropper at a time to each one. After the initial trial run they soon learned to lick from the dropper, and also, which is very important, not to fight each other for the feeder. It was relative child's play to administer a dropperful to one baby and leave him slowly to digest the food whilst administering a dropperful to the next baby. And so it went on.

On the whole the Bushbabies behaved a little more rationally than the squirrels, who tended to be greedy little creatures. By contrast, the baby Bushbabies adored lying in your hand and, when they had had enough, would nod off, still clutching the end of the dropper with their pink hands. In this way it was fairly easy to regulate the feeding. Unhappily, not all baby mammals are like this; a lot of them tend to be greedy and will go on taking as much food as you choose to give them, which could literally be fatal. Gerry had warned me about this danger, citing the case of his own sister Margaret, who, when left to look after a family of baby hedgehogs, did not heed Gerry's warning that they were greedy and were only to be fed a certain amount each meal time. She fondly believed that, as they were squeaking their heads off after the allotted amount of food, they must be desperately hungry. So she fed them, and fed them, and fed them until they literally died of over-eating. Some people might say this would be a lovely way to die, but I don't recommend the technique as a way of keeping an animal in good health.

You can only learn by trial and error how much food should be administered, but on the whole I found that three eye-droppers full of the rather rich mixture which we habitually used and which I described on p. 99 was more than enough at a session. We used the same mixture, together with chopped meat, fruit and bread, for all our mammals and they all throve on it. We have since done the same with great success here in the zoo, for everything from the smallest bird to the largest mammal, and although it is a rather expensive mixture to indulge in, if you are seriously considering keeping exotic species, it is an excellent basic diet.

My little colony of Demidoff's flourished so that eventually, in the enormous room which I had converted into a nursery, there was the Tilley heater throwing its beautiful red warm glow on to biscuit boxes full of Demidoff's, three different types of squirrel, a couple of baby monkeys, a baby Palm Civet and the little mice which Gerry simply could not resist. They all came to recognize us and were not a bit frightened when a large and often damp hand was inserted into their cosy nests in order to bring them out for feeding. I tried not to wait until they were squealing for food, but did, whenever possible, keep to a definite feeding routine. When very small, I fed the creatures hourly, increasing the feeding limit as they grew older and stronger.

Not all the animals kept a rapport with us once they had grown up. They seemed suddenly to relish their independence and not to want to remember their once total reliance on another animal species. This was particularly evident in some of the monkeys, who behaved as though we had had nothing to do with them when young. Yet there were the other creatures, and in particular the Spot-nosed Monkey, 'Miffy', and the Mona Monkey, 'Brownie', who never relished the idea of becoming adult. Whenever they wanted to attract attention the Mona would scream her head off, for no apparent reason, and refuse to stop until you picked her up and cuddled her. This could be very wearing indeed, for there are few things worse than a Monkey screeching endlessly at the top of its voice. The Spot-nosed Monkey, on the other hand, several times feigned to be near death, lying inert at the bottom of his cage. This had us in panic before we realized that all he wanted was to be made much of. It took him quite a while to realize that we had tumbled to this ruse; he was most put out when it finally dawned on him that we were not to be further deceived.

Another problem with hand-rearing a creature is to get it to accept the idea of feeding itself without either drowning itself in the milk or getting a piece of fruit stuck in the throat. Here again, I found monkeys to be stupid in comparison to the smaller mammals, who seemed to want to chew and gnaw at things as soon as they possibly could. There was another little Mona Monkey which, when presented with a dish of milk, promptly submerged its entire face and came up a spluttering, soggy mass. This particular monkey *never* really learnt to lap milk properly and had to be helped to feed until we could get a drip type of feeder which, when sucked, released milk automatically into its waiting mouth. Happily, this was our only failure which, when you consider we had roughly 350 animals all told, including reptiles, was a measure of the success of our methods.

Unlike most females, I am addicted to mice. I realize that this word often conjures up an unpleasant image, but I do maintain that closer acquaintanceship with mice reveals their endearing qualities, which the story of Bertram, the dormouse, illustrates perfectly.

In looks Bertram's family closely resemble the common European dormice but they are more silvery-grey in colour and have a bushier tail. We had had this particular colony of dormice for some time and they had all lived together in perfect accord and had given us a great deal of pleasure watching their acrobatic displays each night. There was one that we could always distinguish, for he had a tiny white star on his flank, also he was a much better athlete than the others, so that his daring leaps and somersaults had earned our admiration. This was the reason we decided to call him Bertram Mills, or Bertram for short.

The chimpanzee, Chumley, with nothing else to do, naturally got up to mischief. One of the boys had not realized the close proximity of Chumley's box to the dormouse cage. One evening there was a large crash and the poor little dormice, who had been sleeping happily, were thrown together with their cage on to the floor. By the time we arrived, they were rushing around frantically, Chumley, 'ooooing' with delight and trying to catch them. By the time Chumley had been secured and dealt with, there was not a dormouse in sight; funnily enough not because they had tried to escape, but because they believed that sleep was the most important thing in their lives, and so they had leapt behind the cages to find suitable slumbering spots.

The fact that the entire collection had eventually to be moved so as to enable us to recapture the dormice did not really improve our tempers. The only dormouse that proved to be difficult to catch, however, was naturally Bertram. This was a perfect opportunity for him to show off his prowess and he proceeded to leap and do somersaults and lightning turns as we pursued him frantically around the room. Gerry kept screaming to us all: 'For heavens' sake remember the tail, don't catch it by the tail,' but it was to no avail; one of the boys, seeing Bertram disappear behind another row of cages, grabbed him by the only part of his anatomy that was visible. The result was predictably disastrous; the fine skin on the tail broke away and peeled off, like the finger of a glove.

This could be a defence mechanism, similar to that used by lizards, who drop their tail when caught by an enemy. Bertram was eventually recaptured and examined carefully. An interesting fact about animals is that, when they sustain an injury, however ghastly it might look to us, they generally seem to be completely unconcerned. This was certainly the case with Bertram, who sat primly in Gerry's hand, almost unaware of what had happened to him. Nothing we could do could save the tail itself because, deprived of its outer layer of skin, the bone would eventually wither, dry and then break off. This left the dormouse none the worse off, except that, in Bertram's case, his tail was essential to his balance during his acrobatics. As he was particularly agile we hoped that he would overcome this handicap in time, but we feared that the psychological adjustment would be painful.

After long consultation, we decided that the kindest thing to do would be to amputate the tail, using anaesthetics, and then to let him go. This we did amongst the luxuriant bougainvillea which festooned the Fon's rest house. Bertram looked delightful sitting on the bougainvillea stem, clutching it tightly with his little pink paws, whiskers quivering. He made no attempt to run off and hide amongst the bougainvillea, as we had expected him to do. Instead, after a slight pause to regain his equilibrium, he leapt down on to the veranda rail, then on to the floor, and scurried across to the line of cages against the far wall. Gerry immediately retrieved him and returned him to the bougainvillea, but as soon as he was released he did exactly the same thing again. Time after time we tried to persuade him that we really did not want him any more and that the bougainvillea was to be his new home, but quite unsuccessfully. Eventually, we all got a bit fed up with this so we put him once more in the creeper and left him to it, thinking that he would eventually go off.

Later that evening, when we came to giving the dormice their fresh food for the night, we discovered a most unusual spectacle. On top of the dormouse cage was the bundle of cotton waste which we used as bedding, changing the damp wool as and when it became too unhygienic. That evening, we decided it was a clean bed night all round, so removing the weird collection of trophies that dormice always seem to assemble in their bedrooms, we pulled out the dirty cotton waste, grabbing a new piece to replace it. As Gerry seized the bundle of waste, he was unexpectedly and sharply bitten in the thumb. He made a lot of loud noises and danced around waving his hand in the air. It must have been a shock for, after all, you do not expect cotton waste suddenly to turn round and bite you. We rushed over to see what had happened and carefully examined what was left of the cotton waste, whereupon a little, fat face peeped out of the middle. It was Bertram, chittering and squeaking in an indignant manner. By this time, Gerry was very annoyed indeed, and so he hauled him out of his cosy nest and plonked him in the bougainvillea again. Bertram spent a good half-hour chittering and chattering at us in order to retain his dignity and his rights, but by dinner time he was back where he had started, in the bundle of cotton waste. Being too weary to go on struggling with him we went off and had our dinner.

It was our normal practice, just before going to bed, to do a last minute check to make sure that the animals were happy, no ants were around and, generally, just to say goodnight to them. As we got to the dormouse cage, all the residents came rushing out of their bedrooms and pounced upon their food plates with squeaks of anticipation. There, hanging on the wire, peering wistfully at the food and the other dormice so obviously enjoying their suppers, was Bertram. He looked so pathetic hanging there watching the others with their delicious tit-bits that we surrendered and gave him a plate of food on the top of the cage.

This went on for some considerable time until in the end he wore us down completely. We realized that the only way we would get any peace was to put him back in the cage. What alternative was there? The animal refused to be released so we just had to keep him.

Bertram did not seem to suffer in any way from the loss of his tail; in fact, if my memory serves me right, I seem to have detected in him a slightly superior attitude towards the others. He had, after all, completely defeated the intentions of those who flattered themselves that they were the most superior animals. No wonder that he considered he should now be treated in a more deferential manner than hitherto by his fellow dormice.

We are often asked about the problems of transporting animals from their country of origin back to the British Isles. Without doubt, this is the most harrowing part of any trip. On the whole, there are no dangers involved in actually catching and maintaining animals. Such perils as are encountered are generally due to one's own stupidity or ignorance or, as sometimes happened in our case, to the actions of human beings over whom we had no control. Speaking personally, the worries of the journey back often completely outweighed the enjoyment of the actual trip itself. I love to travel and to meet people, and I love, even more, meeting the strange and bizarre creatures that inhabit the various countries we visit, but I loathe the nervous tension involved in bringing back a collection of animals.

I have seen the results of the handling of animals by certain animal dealers and I would be ashamed even to think of using their methods. I remember once witnessing – in South America – a truck laden with animal crates speeding along the highway to the local airport. When it was forced to brake hard, one of the crates broke loose and fell to the ground. It split open to reveal hundreds of Black-headed Parakeets, wedged together in this small box. I was horrified, but then delighted when most of those that were still alive flew away. We had stopped, naturally, to help, and I feel sure that if it had not been for our presence, a lot of badly injured parakeets would have been repacked and left to die. As it was, we helped to dispatch them as humanely as possible. I have seen other instances where dealers have used the most barbaric methods, not only to catch but to ship animals. I see no justification for this. Of course, by giving one's animals adequate accommodation for the trip, the right food and travel at a slower pace, one is going to use more money. If one is only in the business in order to make money, the dealers would argue that our methods are impossible. This, alas, seems to be true. Certainly *we* have never yet made any money collecting animals. It is only by the books that we write that we manage to survive at all. Our present trips are now confined to special rescue operations, to catch and bring back to Jersey animals that are faced with total extinction in their natural habitats, so that we may breed and save them.

Throughout our travels we have been very lucky that almost everyone with whom we have come into contact has been as anxious as we are to preserve the animals and to make sure that they arrive at their destination in as perfect a condition as possible. I think that our methods have vindicated themselves because not only have we had animals land in marvellous condition, but we have even bred animals in these travelling boxes. Most of our boxes have had, where possible, a secluded sleeping compartment and by carrying this method through to our keeping of animals here in Jersey, we have found that it is highly successful. An animal simply must feel secure, otherwise it will not be happy and certainly will not breed.

Gerry's principal ambition had always been to have a zoo of his own, and in order to give us some real objective, we had decided that the animals collected on this trip to West Africa should form the nucleus of such a zoo. We argued, and I think quite rightly, that a zoo in the Bournemouth area was needed. The nearest zoos at that time were Bristol in the west and London to the north, so there was a vast area unserved. According to family legend, Gerry had spent every minute (before I married him and when he first inherited his money) looking for a suitable property, and I remember his sister despairing of ever getting Gerry to go anywhere that did not have a zoo site at the end of it. Perhaps if we now appeared in Bourne-mouth with our collection of animals we might be able to put pressure on either the local corporation or some local wealthy person, who might offer us a suitable property. In return, we offered a collection of rare and unusual creatures to form a perfect basis for any zoological collection. Gerry had his expertise and I had a modicum of business training, so perhaps we could help with the administration and the general day-to-day care of the animals.

It was with this somewhat hazy vision that we con-fidently arrived in Bournemouth. We were greeted by my sister-in-law Margaret with what, I am sure, were mixed feelings. She, like the rest of the family, had always rather doted on Gerry and shared his wild enthusiasm for animals and so it did not take much to persuade her to allow us to occupy her garage and large back garden. With the help of a friend we converted the garage into a 'hot' area for those animals that needed constant heat, and on the back lawn, erected a large square marquee brought back from Africa.

To begin with, our neighbours were sympathetic and friendly, that is until it became obvious that our problem was not going to be easily solved and that no one was eager to offer us a site. The Bournemouth Corporation were hardly progressive in their outlook, and despite much mouthing of sympathy and interest, we did not get any concrete assistance from them. However, the local Poole Corporation, which had rather unwillingly been saddled with a property on the edge of Poole harbour, offered this as a possibility. To begin with our negotiations with them went extremely well and it was agreed that they would let us have the property on a long lease whilst we would furnish the initial capital.

Contrary to popular belief best-selling authors, on the whole, do not make an awful lot of money, unless their book happens to be taken by a film company who wish to make it into a mammoth production. Also, the word 'best-selling' is misleading. Whereas in the old days, if you were a best-selling author you sold literally hundreds of thousands of copies, these days, if you sell fifty thousand copies in hard-back, you are regarded as being a great success. So although Gerry's books had, happily, provided enough finance to keep us and enable us to go on collecting trips, we had not been able to save any money and were leading a book-to-mouth existence. At our bank in London was an extremely sympathetic manager, who shared our view that a zoo was a good idea and was even more interested in our eventual purpose of turning what, we hoped, was going to be a successful zoo, into an equally successful charitable trust, on the lines of Peter Scott's Wildfowl Trust in Slimbridge. He took not long to convince that we were worth investing in and so it was agreed, with our publisher acting as guarantor, that the bank would loan us £10,000; in 1957 not an inconsiderable sum. This meant, of course, that we were mortgaging ourselves up to the hilt, we owned no property and had no other security but Gerry's ability.

I think it was a measure of our bank manager's regard for Gerry that he was prepared to recommend the loan on this basis.

Negotiations with the Poole Council dragged on and soon it became obvious that the conditions they wished to impose in any final agreement were absolutely out of the question. I lost my patience and became very irritated; it seemed that the day of private initiative was over and that in order to get anything done as an individual, mountains of red tape had to be overcome. Life was far too short and in the meantime our animals had to be fed, our irate neighbours objected to the continued presence of wild animals in their midst, and, what was even more worrying, winter was coming on. Paignton Zoo came to our rescue by offering to house most of the creatures, on the firm understanding that they would be removed by a certain date. If we were unable to remove them they would become the property of the zoo. On the surface this seemed a little harsh, but we were stuck for any other solution and had to accept.

Our determination to find a suitable site grew until, in an inspired moment, I suggested to Gerry that it might be a good idea to look further afield, to somewhere that was still within the British sphere of influence and yet where it might be possible to get decisions fairly rapidly. After a great deal of thought it became obvious that the only place that adequately met all our needs was Jersey in the Channel Islands. Although we had never been there ourselves friends had, and all spoke glowingly of it, particularly of its weather. Rupert Hart-Davis, then our publisher, who had been enthusiastic about our ideas from the first, had a friend in Jersey and suggested that we contact him and perhaps go over to see the island. Our difficulties were becoming even more acute by this time; not only had we had to find a home for the animals but we also had to go on another trip so as to get material to write a further book, in order to survive. This ghastly squirrel-in-a-wheel complex has dogged our existence from the very beginning.

Grasping the opportunity offered by Hart-Davis, we eventually turned up in Jersey to be met by Major Fraser, who kindly escorted us round the island and took us back to his own property at Les Augres Manor for lunch. The manor itself was a perfect setting for a zoo. It was a charming old granite house with lovely arches, having been an old fortified farm. The many granite outbuildings lent themselves ideally to conversion. Imagine our delight when it turned out that Hugh Fraser himself was wanting to leave the island and to let the property. It seemed almost too good to be true.

It soon became obvious why Hugh had been a major in the Guards. No sooner had we decided that his was a perfect place, than he immediately set in motion everything which led to our ultimate success. The then head of tourism was the late Senator Wilfred Krichefski. He was a man of tremendous energy and foresight and, happily for us, at once saw the tourist potential offered by such a scheme. Fired with enthusiasm, which was obviously transmitted to every department in the States of Jersey, he ensured that within three weeks we had accomplished what had proved to be impossible in the United Kingdom. We had found the site, got permission and started to build.

A friend, who had had zoo experience, took over the supervision of the initial building of the zoo so that we would be free to go to South America and collect more animals.

The people of Jersey, from the start, have always welcomed both us and our endeavours, and our success has been due, in no small way, to the continual encouragement that we have always received from them and their government.

We ran it as a straightforward zoo until 1963, when the sale of one of Gerry's books to a film company enabled us to discharge our then indebtedness of £25,000 plus, to the bank. Then Gerry launched on the final phase of his treasured ambition; the creation of a scientific charitable trust where animals in danger of extinction could be kept, studied and bred, in the hope that, by so doing, not only would we save them from extinction but also, at some future date, perhaps re-introduce them into their original habitat.

This sounds a wild and unrealistic idea, but since the creation of the Trust in 1963 it has become a more and more vital link in the whole conservation picture. That people do now consider that it is important to conserve wild things and wild places is gratifying, not only because of their commercial value, but because we have no right to decimate the wild creatures that share our planet. As Gerry often remarks: 'No one would dare destroy a Rembrandt, so why destroy one of God's creations?' With the help of a small, enthusiastic band of people in Jersey, we established here what is now a unique organization – one whose total resources are devoted to the cause of wildlife conservation, by controlled breeding of endangered species.

It was inevitable that, when undertaking a scheme of this magnitude, we had to be more selective in the choice of our animals and to concentrate on small nuclei of endangered species. This is how N'Pongo the gorilla came to us. In 1962, we had a telephone call from an English animal dealer. There was a young female Lowland Gorilla for sale on the Continent. Would we be interested? There never has been a time when we had any spare cash, but at that moment we were particularly short. Gerry, however, always refused to accept lack of finance as a real obstacle to achieving anything, which is just as well, because if he had been daunted by poverty, we would never have achieved a single thing – not even marriage. He said 'yes' to the dealer, then tackled the problem of raising the cash.

After a lot of thought one possible solution emerged; at least, he thought it was possible, although I admit at the time I was very pessimistic. He argued that there were more wealthy people to the square inch in Jersey than anywhere else in the world and it just might intrigue some of them to be offered a part of a gorilla, a sort of hire purchase scheme. Having contacted a couple of friends for names of possible victims, he settled down by the telephone and proceeded to make a series of calls. Most people were so intrigued by the idea that eventually he got the money, one person even offering to put up the entire balance.

So it was a joyful Mr Durrell who flew over to London Airport. Excitedly, he rang us from there, saying it was indeed a baby Lowland Gorilla and absolutely adorable. We were at the airport when he got back and for the first time met N'Pongo. On the drive to the zoo she merely sat on Gerry's lap watching the countryside and the Jersey cows pass by. Her quarters were not quite ready, so she was installed in our flat in the Manor House. After our experiences with chimpanzees, who are ebullient creatures, N'Pongo's gravity and extremely decorous behaviour completely won over everyone who came into contact with her. She took to flat-living without a qualm. There was no attempt to break anything or to misbehave in any other way, even when she occasionally walked round the room to examine things she did so very carefully. N'Pongo was such a success that Gerry's mother, who was living with us by then, was quite prepared to have her as a permanent member of the household. However, after our experiences with Chumley in Bournemouth, we put our foot down. We said it was all right as a temporary measure but as small gorillas had a habit of becoming big gorillas, and might not be quite so trustworthy, it was not to be encouraged.

N'Pongo's relationship with our boxer dog, Keeper, was most amusing. Keeper I had got as an adult dog and he had never known anything like a zoo before. In fact he had been brought up in a council house, confined to a back garden and a small kitchen, but he took to his new life with such gay abandon that everyone was under the impression that we had had him from a small puppy.

To avoid misunderstandings, we had evolved a definite arrangement with Keeper. He was introduced properly to any animal that we brought into the flat and allowed to smell it for a little while, then told, very firmly, that this creature was 'no', by which he knew we meant it was not to be molested in any way. Keeper was an extremely well-mannered dog and never at any time took liberties with any creature that we presented to him in this way. His one good friend was Claudius our South American Tapir, whom he visited regularly every day so that they could lick each other's nose through the wire barrier. This worked very satisfactorily until Keeper got carried away one day and forgot to move his tongue quickly enough. Claudius, forever in pursuit of the edible, thought 'Ah, tasty tit-bit', and nipped his friend's tongue smartly. The poor dog was quite hurt by this sudden attack, although Claudius, I am sure, did not mean any harm, being quite as dim-witted as Keeper. The incident caused a rift in their friendship for a couple of days, but after that, I think Keeper realized, dimly, that no offence had been meant and so resumed his daily visits.

N'Pongo intrigued Keeper, and he would smell her, then try to lick her. N'Pongo loved this great ginger dog and would pat him and pull at him a bit, but not at all viciously; it was more like a small child would behave except that N'Pongo was far more gentle than the average child would have been.

At that time, one of the staff had a small daughter. She and N'Pongo became good friends and they loved nothing better than to sit in the middle of the room, back to back, like a couple of bookends, pensively looking at a piece of food that they were sharing or studying a picture book that the little girl had brought in to show her friend. It was a charming relationship and I am sure that everyone who met this young gorilla fell similarly under her spell. Certainly she succeeded in captivating Jeremy Mallinson, Gerry's second-in-command, who adored her from the moment he set eyes on her, and still maintains a tremendous rapport with her, even though she is now fourteen years old and has two children.

I cannot remember any animal whom I was more sad to see leave our flat. I do not feel this way about all the animals that we have had to infest ourselves with, but N'Pongo was so sweet, so gentle and, above all, so well-mannered. By the time she left us, her cage area had been well prepared and she needed the extra space, plus all the 'furniture' that we had managed to put in – like chains, ropes and logs – so that she could be fully occupied. Apart from this, Jeremy was anyway dying to get his hands on her.

On fine afternoons we would bring her out on to the front lawn and play games with her, which she thoroughly enjoyed. The dog and the little girl joined in and anyone else who could be tempted was welcome. Even to this day, N'Pongo has remained her usual calm, well-mannered self and accepts all the admiration (particularly Jeremy's) that is offered to her, with a regal air.

Chapter Eight

A Dog's Life

Many other strange creatures have shared our private life and I would not like to neglect three more, all totally different but each with its own special characteristics.

One brief visitor was Dingle, the chough. He belonged to a lady who lived in Dorset. She apparently had had him for many years and he had become ridiculously tame, in fact frighteningly so, because he was unaware of any threat from anything or anybody, dogs, cats, or even more important, human beings. She had kept him in the house for some time, but, unfortunately, one day he had taken it into his head to go wandering off. The next thing she heard was that someone had found him, badly injured, having been attacked by some unthinking children. He fortunately recovered but later wandered off again and the same thing happened.

By this time, the poor woman was getting desperate. Being an avid reader of Gerry's books, she felt that we perhaps could offer Dingle the sort of life that he would enjoy; we might even be able to get him a mate, although choughs are now extremely rare. We offered to do what we could for him. We drove over to her house to collect him and he behaved beautifully.

Fortunately, he liked us and soon settled down; he was, like all choughs, very inquisitive, and stalked around the room digging his beak into everything he could find. One of his favourite habits was to sit on top of one's head and poke around in one's hair, as though looking for worms or the odd insect. This was tolerable; it became a little much though when he started digging round your ears. Again, Keeper accepted him without a word and, although he had the odd dig at Keeper with his beak, the boxer never retaliated or inflicted upon him the indignities that other creatures had done.

At this time we also had a bushbaby. This creature had come to us from a lady who could no longer keep him. She was moving house and her new neighbours did not really care to have a wild animal living next door. He, too, had been used to freedom since he had lived in the house and done virtually what he wanted. She begged us to take him and in the end we agreed. But we gave way reluctantly because there is always danger inherent in taking over other people's pets; we have had one or two unfortunate experiences in this way.

So it was that 'Mousechew', as he was called, came into our lives. He was relatively well behaved and slept for most of the day but when in the evenings we would let him out he would bounce all round the room with arms outstretched, his eyes bulging with curiosity. A disarming but rather disconcerting habit of his was suddenly to bounce up beside you on a chair or settee and his abrupt appearance startled many a visitor. However, his favourite trick was to wait until a vase of flowers appeared, to creep up (unnoticed, of course, by us), part the flowers and slowly submerge the whole of his body in the water, clinging to the side and peering over the edge of the vase. Why he indulged in this habit none of us ever knew, but he used to emerge, soaking wet, and proceed to jump over the furniture and against the walls so that our lovely white walls soon became festooned with little black fingermarks.

He became even more of a problem because he would bounce up and down in front of Keeper until the poor dog was driven almost mad. Then his attention turned to Dingle, who, however, soon got the measure of him and tried pecking his eyes out. It became obvious that life was becoming intolerable for all three animals. With a heavy heart we decided that we had better go back to being a normal household. Dingle was put in an aviary with some other birds, and seemed well contented with a daily visit from us and a head scratch. Mousechew was placed in one of the bigger cages with some more bushbabies and reverted to being quite normal. Keeper, with a sigh of relief, resumed his normal behaviour pattern of eating, lolling in front of the fire and pottering around the zoo, stopping only to say 'good-morning' to Claudius.

It is lovely having animals living with you, but we feel that, in fairness to them, it is essential that they should have a definite routine. It is also unwise to inflict one's own routine on animals; the best thing is that they should evolve their own. One creature that we did have in the flat who utterly refused to be influenced by us in any way at all, was Whiskers, the Emperor Tamarin. Whiskers is a magnificent creature, being very attractive to look at and getting his name from the enormous white moustache which makes him look like Kaiser Bill. Gerry had always had a passion for these little primates from South America, since the days before the war when he had had a black-headed Marmoset as a pet. They are bird-like in character and fearless, a rule to which Whiskers was no exception.

He arrived in pathetically bad condition (from a dealer, of course) and was obviously suffering from the cage paralysis that often afflicts these South American primates. With the help of our veterinary friend in Bournemouth, we had evolved a perfect answer, but unfortunately, it involved a massive injection of vitamins D and B12. No one liked administering these injections, but unfortunately, if the animals were to be saved, there was no alternative. Poor old Whiskers was given the shot. Unlike others of his species who accepted it philosophically and did not connect the pain with the person who was giving the injection, he immediately turned round, looked at Gerry, and bit him severely on the hand; a warning as to what would happen if he was to try to repeat the operation. Gerry was so amused and taken aback that all he could do was laugh. This pugnacity was characteristic of Whiskers; later he became, for his size (a mere six inches), one of the most ferocious specimens in the zoo. If he adored you, you were fine, but if he did not, he would leap upon your head and try to bite you viciously.

As he was in such a weakened condition when he arrived, it was decided to keep him in the flat for a little while, in order to build up his strength. At this time our Common Marmosets had a youngster who was approximately the same size as Whiskers and so they were brought up as companions. They spent most of their day in a large cage in Gerry's mother's bedroom. She, of course, doted on them. Nothing was too much trouble. She would spend two hours every morning cooking delicacies for them, stewing apples with honey or brown sugar, boiling rice and lentils, making other little tit-bits that she was sure they would like. Of course, this was entirely the wrong treatment for Whiskers and, from being naturally arrogant, he became unbearable. He refused to go into his cage until he wanted to, and he and his friend Popadum tore round poor Mrs Durrell's bedroom, rioted over the bed, played havoc with her possessions and really completely took her over. They did have their moments of rest when they would sit calmly in her lap, but most of the time they were tearing her knitting out of her hand, hiding her wool, getting in and out of her knitting bag, strewing bits of wool and patterns all over the place – in fact, becoming totally unmanageable.

Gerry's mother had never really been noted for the

viciousness of her nature, or the sternness of her discipline, and it became obvious that the sooner we could remove these two monsters from her care, the better it would be for everyone concerned. Strangely enough, when the time came, Whiskers accepted his new accommodation with great aplomb and soon asserted his domination over his cage companions. Unhappily, we have never managed, throughout the years, to find him a mate. This is not for want of trying, because we have a file as thick as a loaf of bread relating to Whiskers and his marital problems. We hope and pray that we will eventually find one before Whiskers is too old to appreciate her and before he forgets that the whole purpose in being here is in order to breed.

Whiskers still holds court every morning and, when he sees anyone he knows, pushes out his tongue, wags it furiously and squeaks. If you are tempted to put your finger in to tickle him it can be dangerous. Depending on the mood that he is in (and he is a capricious creature) he will either accept your attention condescendingly or, more often than not, whip round suddenly in an effort to bite you.

Since my first trip in 1954, I have naturally become deeply involved with many animals, but there has never been any one creature that meant so much to me as Timothy, the West African Ground Squirrel.

It has been our practice over the years to make trips, whenever possible, to other zoos, particularly the ones in Europe. Whilst we are in these places we visit the leading dealers, just in case they might have something interesting. I do not enjoy these visits, because dealers in the main do not give the care and attention to their stock that I would like. A few do but, unhappily, they are rare. Nevertheless, they quite often have things we want. It was during one such trip to Holland that we got Timothy.

In the course of conversation with a zoo Director, Gerry happened to mention that I personally was particularly interested in small mammals. Our friend promised faithfully that should anything like this come to his notice he would let us know immediately. We gave him the name of our hotel, just in case he unearthed a contact before we left.

Back at the hotel that evening, we had a telephone call from the Director to say that, strangely enough, that very afternoon a seaman had approached him with several things he thought he might like to buy, amongst which was a very tame squirrel. It was a youngster but he felt that perhaps it might be just what we were looking for. Gerry arranged that the sailor would come and see him at the hotel later. By this time I was practically falling asleep over my food and went off to bed, leaving Gerry to wait for our visitor. I had just dropped off into a sound sleep when the telephone rang shrilly in my ear – it was Gerry.

'You don't feel like coming down?' he asked.

'No, I don't,' I told him firmly.

'It's a pity, because this man has got the most

delightful squirrel and I'm sure you'd love it. It's sitting in the middle of the table at the moment eating a lump of sugar and it really is captivating. You're sure you wouldn't like to come down and see it?'

The thought of getting out of my lovely warm bed, clambering into clothes and being polite to a complete stranger was too much.

'If it's really as special as all that, Gerry, for heaven's sake buy it,' I said, and went off to sleep again.

Next morning I woke up to the familiar smell of stale fruit in my nostrils and suddenly realized that it was coming from a little box on the table near the bed. Carefully I went over and peered in. I could not see much, unfortunately, because it was a gloomy box with only a little bit of wire gauze on the front. By this time, Gerry was awake.

'You must see this creature, he's absolutely enchanting,' he said. 'We'll order breakfast and then, when we've got that out of the way I'll let you have a look at him.'

After breakfast, Gerry carefully moved the box over to the light. This movement was greeted by a little growl from inside.

'It doesn't sound tame to me,' I said.

'Oh, it's all right, he's just frightened. You'd be frightened too wouldn't you, if you suddenly woke up in a strange place and were mysteriously moved around? Anyway, you're supposed to like squirrels.'

Apparently the seaman had got the squirrel in

West Africa as a baby and had hand-reared him. Now back home, he found that living with his parents and a squirrel presented difficulties and he'd gone to the zoo Director in the hope that he would take the creature off his hands.

It was obvious that this particular squirrel just did not want to know me. Fresh food and paper were allowed into the box, but no other overtures were permitted. I carried the box on my lap during the car trip home and all we heard was occasional scratching. No attempt to get out and no distress calls. Arriving in Jersey we found a temporary cage and left him alone for the night.

Gerry reminded me that we had actually had one of this species of squirrel when we had been in the Cameroons but, as the poor thing was half dead when it arrived, it had never really had a chance to survive. This type of squirrel was difficult to rear, in particular because they were largely insectivorous and their diet, therefore, posed some rather tricky problems. However, being arrogant about the breed by this time, I decided that no squirrel was going to be too difficult for me to rear and I solemnly informed my husband of this fact. I argued that, if I had managed to rear such a wide selection of small mammals, this one should not present all that much difficulty. I got a very sceptical look from my beloved.

In order really to look at this squirrel we tipped him out into the middle of the living-room carpet. He was not very striking to look at, being mainly sandy in colour with coarse fur and a white stripe down each side. The bright eyes were surrounded by a white circle but it was the tail that was the most startling feature, being brindled on the outside with a broad orange centre piece. I learnt later that this was a key to how Timothy was feeling. If the tail was all fluffed out it meant that he was going to be up to some mischief, but if it was nice and sleek he was going to behave himself. Our first meeting, eye to eye, was not all that successful, he was obviously very nervous. We never forced ourselves upon him, but slowly he became tame and soon emerged as the character of which Gerry had seen some slight hint on that first evening.

To say that he ruled everyone, including the dog, was putting it mildly. He took over our rather large living-room as his territory. Although he had his own quarters, it was when we allowed him out in the afternoons that he came into his own. It did not take him long to realize that our main activity there took place from 5 p.m. onwards, the rest of the day being spent in and around the zoo grounds. So, deliberately, he changed his whole living pattern and became seminocturnal. He woke up in the mornings when I cleaned out the cage and presented him with his new food. This was mainly our highly successful Humming Bird mixture plus brown bread, the odd grape and succulent things like tangerines, but his main joy was mealworms. These are a cannon in the armoury of any animal keeper: I do not know where they originally came from, but they are without doubt the main source of protein available to keepers of all living creatures. They are easily bred and not at all nauseating.

For mealworms, Timothy would do anything. He had six of these fatty creatures every day, which he ate noisily and greedily. He had obviously not been taught as a young squirrel that you do not eat with your mouth open nor make smacking and sucking noises, but somehow or other, all this vulgarity seemed part of his character. I suppose he really was a vulgar squirrel and that is probably why I liked him; I have never been attracted to the prissy, the sleek or the conventional. His idea of a blissful existence was tearing round the room at a speed I have never seen equalled, leaping from side to side and up into the air like a rodeo horse and literally cracking his bushy tail; stalking our mats and, if possible, pouncing on the fringes and pulling at the wool; stalking my hand, which he did extremely well, with three steps forward and two steps back, eventually leaping on to it.

He would sit outwardly peaceful, on my shoulder, watching television avidly until, becoming bored, he would decide that it would be a good idea if I paid him a little more attention. Then he would nip my rather large ear, or my mouth or nose, whichever happened to be the nearest to him at the time. Realizing that he might be stirring up trouble he would scoot away like mad before I could do anything or even open my mouth. If this failed to get a response he would try to climb down the front of my sweater – this was easy to do as most of my sweaters at that time were in fact V-necks. If I happened to be sitting down, he liked nothing better than to roll himself up into a tight ball and urinate profusely, covering us both in a warm flow. Then he would lie there in this soggy area, occasionally nibbling at me, so that I ended up with a wardrobe full of holey sweaters.

I think perhaps the most blissful thing, as far as Timmy was concerned, was to lie on his back in my hands while I tickled him. This he would tolerate until he was almost hysterical and reached the limits of his endurance. Then he would leap out of my hands, like a spring, and rush off, flicking his tail madly, to have a breather. A few minutes later he would worry me to have another tickling session. If I was not prepared to do this, he hoped that I would at least offer him one hand instead, which he would cling on to whilst I tickled him with a finger.

I think it was poor old Keeper who suffered the most from Timothy's presence. Keeper's permanent position, when in the flat, was lying spread-eagled in front of the fire. Timothy too, enjoyed being recumbent in the same spot. The fact that Keeper was lying there did not deter him in the slightest. He just draped himself over the dog's back, back legs dangling over one side, front legs dangling over the other, and head resting on the front paws so that he was in a perfect position to get the maximum heat with the least discomfort. How Keeper tolerated this creature, I do not know.

Getting bored with lying there doing nothing,

Timothy would then scrabble through Keeper's fur hunting for the odd flea, which he thoroughly relished, and scrunching it up noisily. Even after several failures he would go on searching through the fur, because, after all, one never knew what one would find. I do not think Keeper really minded this, indeed I think he realized that in fact Timothy was doing him a favour, but he did get cross when Timothy, getting bored with everything and everybody, would stalk Keeper's foot and bite him suddenly on the paw or (worse still) on his genitalia. For this, Gerry really used to admonish him. It was strange that Timothy always realized that Gerry was the leader of the pack. He tolerated Gerry (just) but he respected him, for he knew that there were limits beyond which he could not go. One of these limits was strictly set to his constant teasing of Keeper. I do not think Timothy was vicious, he was just playful and he could not understand why this large, lumbering creature would not join in a game with him. The fact that, owing to his good nature, Keeper restrained himself from biting his persecutor, never seemed to occur to Timothy. He certainly never realized how dangerous a threat Keeper could have been if he had been a bad-tempered or even a normal dog.

When Keeper was not in the room, Tim would 'kipper' himself, as a friend called it, in front of the fire; he would sprawl, legs outstretched at the back, arms at the front and then he would yawn deeply, a large, long pink tongue curling out, and doze. After a while he would sit up and have a little scratch.

His favourite posture was one which I could never resist. He would sit bolt upright on his hind legs, front paws dangling in front, looking cheekily round to see what mischief he could get up to. He loved paper and if he found the *Radio Times* or another magazine he would dash madly round the room with it, knocking over everything as he passed. Totally undaunted by its size he would then try and stuff the whole lot into his cage. Many a time we have had to retrieve some newly-arrived magazine from his teeth.

Another favourite device for catching our attention was to leap up on one of the easy chairs or the settee and start scratching madly at the cushions. This, he knew, would bring the wrath of Gerry on him. It was almost as though he was daring Gerry to deal with him. We were never forced to get really tough with Timmy, however, for he knew that if we shouted 'Timothy' in a very stern voice that this was a warning to be heeded. But though he would do so, it would only be for about two seconds flat, during which he would stand up on his hind legs and look at us cheekily, with his head cocked on one side.

Tim had several passions in his life. One of them was brandy and Perrier. I often used to have this drink in the evening and he suddenly became addicted to it and would literally fight me to get into the glass. One day, in his eagerness, he practically submerged. As I decided that brandy was perhaps a little too strong for him (making him even more obstreperous than he already was) I eventually persuaded him to drink

Perrier, straight. You only had to take the top off the bottle; when he heard the 'swish' that was enough. He would pursue you round the room until you gave him some.

Another great thing in Timothy's life was Fox's Glacier Mints. One of the boys, who was 'squirrel sitting' for us one evening when we went out to dinner, happened to be eating one of these mints and he described the terrible tussle he had had with Timothy to save some for himself. Thereafter we used to buy him a quarter of a pound of mints every so often and chop one up into little bits which he would lick and lick, noisily and greedily, until it had all disappeared. He even inspected the ends of his claws to make sure a tiny morsel was not hiding there.

Potato crisps were another of the luxuries of life; not all the vulgar, new flavours of course, but the good old-fashioned potato crisp which, again, he would eat noisily. The first time he encountered them we had bought an enormous box of these crisps for a party and thought it would be amusing to put the nearly empty box on the floor to see what he would do with it. At first he regarded it with great apprehension. Slowly and carefully, with his tail fluffed out, fully alert, he approached it on his tummy, edging nearer and nearer, stopping every now and again to look round to make sure an enemy was not approaching. Finally he screwed up enough courage to get to the opening, where the sudden aroma of potato crisps so overcame him that he dashed inside without a second thought. All we could hear were smacking, crunching noises. Eventually he emerged, his whiskers covered in tiny pieces of potato crisp. He was very satisfied with that and slept for at least ten minutes, having devoured all these little bits.

His relationship with Gerry was always one which afforded me great amusement. Gerry adored him almost as much as I did, but as I say, Timothy was well aware that he was the real source of discipline in the house. Timothy would often lie fast asleep in my hands. If Gerry approached to tickle him under the chin with a forefinger Timothy would lie there, apparently accepting him, until suddenly he smelt the nicotine on Gerry's hands or something, for he would wake up with a start and fly out of my hands. Gerry had never done anything to him, but I think Timothy was very wary of him.

Often when staff came up to see Gerry, Timothy would approach them, completely unafraid. If he liked them, then, in his opinion, they could only be there for him to play with. I remember when John Hartley, the Trust Secretary, came up one evening. Sitting down on the floor he had a drink and was talking to Gerry about one thing and another. Suddenly, for no reason at all, Timothy decided that a great game would be to attack John. John has legs at least three times longer than anybody else's and these were elegantly laid across the mat in the centre of the carpet. Timothy devised his own game of tag. He rushed round and round the room, stopping occasionally, leaping at John's trousers, pulling at them and then running away. This went on and on, and nothing we could do could deter him from it. John was extremely patient with him and just laughed. He knew well that Timothy was not doing it viciously but out of devilment. I think Timothy realized that we were all far too engrossed in our conversation to be worried about him and was determined to make his presence felt.

It was surprising to me that an animal with his temperament should not be at all destructive. There was one exception, however, when we had some friends round to dinner. We had all disappeared into the kitchen, leaving Timothy ensconced in the living-room. We had noticed that, whenever the living-room door was left open, Timothy would scamper out to investigate, but that he would soon get frightened and rush, panic-stricken, around in circles until we came to his rescue by herding him back to the living-room, where he felt secure. This evening, we had carefully closed the door behind us, thinking that he had quite enough to occupy himself with. Coming back into the living-room unexpectedly, I found Timothy sitting in the middle of our beautiful new Spanish rug, tearing a large hole in it. He was so startled at my appearance that he merely sat there, large pieces of orange and red wool sticking out of his mouth. I do not know who was more aghast, he or me. Anyway, he shot past me to hide behind the settee and eventually re-appeared, peering warily round the edge of the settee to see what I would do. He knew exactly what he had done; never again did he attack the mats, or indeed anything else.

I have always tried hard not to become too emotionally attached to my pets because, on the whole, they have a fairly short life span in comparison to human beings. To be too involved is inevitably painful. My relationship with Timothy, already dangerously intense, was made still more so when Gerry, who had been grossly overworking, had a total collapse and was ordered to rest. By this, the doctor meant a *complete* rest, away from Jersey, and it was suggested that he spend two or three weeks in a London nursing home, completely divorced from everything to do with the zoo and his other work. I, in the meantime, could not very well leave Timothy or Keeper so I came back to Jersey. For those three weeks I came to rely utterly on the companionship of Keeper, to a lesser degree, but even more, of Timothy. We had such communication that it was as if he knew that he had to be on his best behaviour, to be more amusing, more of a companion than he had ever been. If I did not feel like playing with him he would sit on my lap or curl around my neck. If I felt in the mood for chasing him round the room or allowing him to stalk my hand or to play with the mat, he would respond enthusiastically.

One day he got too exuberant and happened to hit his nose rather hard against one of the wooden table legs. I was horrified to see him suddenly having a sort of convulsion, with blood streaming from his nose.

I gave him some Perrier and held him very quietly. I think he must have given himself slight concussion, because he was quite quiet for the next day or two. I had the vet in immediately to examine him but there appeared to be nothing wrong; his eyesight and everything else seemed to be normal. The vet felt that if I could keep him quiet for a few days more, he would be fine. Needless to say, being Timothy, it did not take him long to get over this attack, but he did at least remember next time not to go too near those very solid legs.

It is always a wrench when one has to go away and leave a favourite animal. Timothy was even more of a problem for we never varied his routine. If we were going to be out for an evening, or were away for long periods, somebody was always there, so that every evening at 5 o'clock his door was opened and out he would come to play and to do all the things that he was used to doing. Everyone said that he missed me when I was away and I think this was only natural, having built up such a great rapport with him, but nevertheless, the staff (who readily agreed to occupy the flat in our absence or sit in of an evening) loved playing with him too, so he was not deprived of companionship.

This happy state of affairs went on for five years. Then, in 1969, we decided that we would go on a six-month trip round Australia. Once again, the problem of Timothy and Keeper presented itself. Keeper by this time was getting old and rather feeble, especially on his back legs, but we were hopeful that, with the care and attention which he got from everyone, he would survive till we returned. Timothy, I was not the slightest bit worried about because he was in the peak of condition. We had left him before for long periods and he had always been his own ebullient self when we got back.

Without any misgivings, we finally sailed to Australia. In a matter of weeks we heard that Keeper had collapsed. I gather there was great mourning in the zoo, for everyone loved Keeper dearly and looked upon him almost as their own property. This, though sad, was not unexpected but the second blow came when I heard that Timothy had died without any warning. Unfortunately, everyone was so upset that no post-mortem was done, so the cause of his death remains a mystery to me. I know from previous experience that squirrels have a tendency to renal failure, and it may well have been this that was the main cause. I do not like to think that it was due to my absence; that he was pining or anything like that. Indeed, I am sure he was not. Probably Timothy lived far longer with me than he would have done either in the wild or, indeed, with his original owner. Throughout his five years with us, he had a marvellous time, he was adored by everyone and I think it came through, very strongly, that here was a very special soul. Being a firm believer in the Buddhist theory that we do not die but merely progress to another life, I like to think that Timothy has gone on to far greater things. It was a great experience for me, and also a tremendous privilege, to have been allowed to share one stage in his development. I do not think there has ever been a squirrel like him, nor do I think there ever will be one again.

Epilogue

What I have tried to do in this book is to show the wide variety of animals that I personally have had to deal with and also to give some idea how their characters differ and the effects that their individual personalities have on the people with whom they come into contact. I hope that I have managed to convey the joy and the delight that I have received through my association with these creatures and that, as a result, you will see and appreciate why my husband particularly, and I incidentally, have decided to dedicate all our resources and all our energies to the preservation of, at least, some of them.

If you feel that you too share our deep concern and would like to help us to help them, please do so by joining the Jersey Wildlife Preservation Trust. We have, at the moment of writing, over 10,000 members, spread all over the world, and through them and our sister organisation, SAFE (Save Animals From Extinction, International) in the United States, we hope and believe that we are spreading the gospel of conservation. It is our aim and ambition that, in future years, we will be able to set up, in various parts of the world, similar organizations to the Trust here in Jersey, where animals can be kept in their country of origin but in a place where they will find true sanctuary, until sanity once more gains a foothold in the world and human beings cease to be totally self-centred and to realize that there are beautiful things for everyone to share. I look forward to hearing from you all and a letter, just addressed to me care of the Trust, Jersey, Channel Islands, will always receive a reply.